When You Have Outgrown Him

When You Have Outgrown Him
Whether to Stay or Go

By Dr. Kimberly Ventus-Darks

New Horizon Press
Far Hills, New Jersey

Dr. Kimberly Ventus-Darks
When You Have Outgrown Him: Whether to Stay or Go
Cover design: Robert Aulicino
Interior design: Susan S. Sanderson

Library of Congress Control Number: 2010925083

ISBN 13: 978-0-88282-320-1
New Horizon Press

Manufactured in the U.S.A.

2014 2013 2012 2011 2010 / 5 4 3 2 1

To God, my Father,
my husband, Derrick, and son, Christian.
I love you all very much!

Author's Note

This book is based on the author's research, personal accounts and clients' real life experiences. In order to protect privacy, names have been changed and identifying characteristics have been altered except for contributing experts. For purposes of simplifying usage, the pronouns his/her and s/he are sometimes used interchangeably. The information contained herein is not meant to be a substitute for professional evaluation and therapy with mental health professionals.

Contents

p151

p176

p185

p209

p215

Our Time

This is a written rededication my husband gave to me after thirteen years of marriage, when I so deeply thought that I had outgrown him.

I remember the day I said "I do"
We were young, in love and full of romance
Our dreams of a life together had finally come true
We had our future ahead of us

It has been 13 years since we have exchanged vows
In that time many things have changed
I have watched you grow from a young woman...
To a special woman
Beautiful, confident, accomplished, wise and spiritual
Are among the many qualities of your being

We've witnessed the birth of our son Christian
Whom I contribute much of his upbringing and
Qualities, to your mothering, teaching and direction
Yes, Kimberly, my love, you are a wonderful mother

So much can be said for us as a couple
We've been through happiness and sadness
We've been friends and lovers
We've lived in good times and bad times

You've believed in me and I have believed in you
The time has come for me to renew my love for you
Never replacing our wedding vows, but adding to them
My words are from my heart:

From this day forward my promise to you is
Change from a good man...to a better man
I do this by stating the following:

I promise…
To take our love to a new level in romance and courtship
To explore new heights of my passion toward you
To make you feel more loved in a warmer way

I promise…
To spiritually navigate our home with the eyes of an eagle
To be there for you when you feel weary…
In need of my shoulder to lean on & my arms to hold you
Never to take for granted what we have in each other

I promise…
To walk with you side by side, not from behind or too far ahead
To rediscover and embrace more of your unique, special character
To join you in growth and prosperity

Our time has come. From this day forward, we will live out our
marriage in every way dreamed or imagined. And I begin this by
writing these words and saying…I love you.

—Derrick Darks

Introduction

The mission of *When You Have Outgrown Him* is to expose, acknowledge and then provide practical solutions for the hidden predicament of women outgrowing their mates. It will address growth issues as they pertain to financial, emotional, cultural and spiritual aspects. We'll discuss what it means to outgrow your mate and how the idea of outgrowth is specific to each individual couple. Together we'll learn how you can analyze your relationships from a fair perspective. Men are not the enemies, but rather possible victims of mothers who raised their children under a very popular trap of *loving their boys but teaching their girls.* Boys who were loved instead of taught become men who are loved and unprepared, because they were never taught. I believe this is one of the major reasons behind why women tend to outgrow their mates. *This is not a self-help book on ways to leave and end your relationship, but instead options will be provided on how to view your relationship from a clear and fair perspective, not guided by emotions and feelings but instead realism, fairness and sound judgment. When You Have Outgrown Him* discusses issues the public is not comfortable exposing. You will learn the questions to consider when determining whether your relationship is as bad as it seems—if it is worth leaving your present mate for a partner who could possibly be worse than your current one. In most cases, you need a little of your mate's laidback personality and he needs a little of your superwoman perspective. Research supports that when the two are mixed together, surprisingly it makes a great balance and therefore a very strong relationship.

Is Your Forty-Two-Year-Old Husband Still Watching Cartoons?

What happens when a woman is forced to ask herself these profound questions: *Why is my forty-two-year-old husband still watching cartoons? What does it mean when I am looking for a second job in the Sunday newspaper and my husband is in the family room playing video games?* Regardless if it is due to the embarrassment of having to admit that you have possibly married a kid at heart or the need to hold on to a piece of a marriage that is falling apart, for many women it is a taboo to think that they may have actually fallen into this relationship dilemma where they have outgrown their mates. Media, talk shows and other popular venues discuss how women are stressed out and unappreciated and that the majority of household obligations and outside necessities have become their sole concern and responsibility. The deeper reason, I believe, behind what is really going on is that in too many relationships today women find that they have outgrown their mates. The media often portrays this dilemma in a comical fashion and does a good job of circling around the problem, without actually confronting it head-on. It is not uncommon to see a television commercial where the wife is cooking dinner, putting a load of clothes in the washing machine and tending to three screaming kids all at the same time. Meanwhile the husband successfully tunes out his family by lying on the couch, watching a football game on TV and yelling at the referee for calling a foul on his home team. As women we recognize in commercials like these analogies to our own lives. What was supposed to be joint responsibility with our mates is clearly unbalanced and dangerously one-sided. Most of us would admit that we can relate to the circumstances, but we have yet to label this problem as a possible stage of outgrowth. Until we recognize and confront the truth about this escalating relationship problem, it will continue to go on mislabeled and unresolved. The only hope we have to mend our stress-filled relationships is to unravel the truth behind why so many women outgrow their mates.

In many cases, outgrowing a mate is a reality that is usually thought about and then quickly ignored. Feelings of stress, frustration and disgust are often experienced early in the relationship and signs of imbalance can be detected in the dating stage. Although a woman may start to feel that there is an imbalance of some sort in her relationship, she quickly ignores what she is feeling, because she thinks that most women feel the exact same way she does and that her feelings of frustration are just part of being in a relationship.

However, outgrowing a mate is one of the most ignored issues facing relationships today. It is different from the other topics that couples are many times forced to confront, such as infidelity, career changes and financial problems. These topics have often been blamed for the failure of once stable relationships. Most women are reluctant to discuss the idea of outgrowing their mates for two reasons: One is because it has not been discussed socially and the truth behind this issue is profoundly unknown and therefore uncomfortable. As a society, we have been guilty of calling this problem the *superwoman syndrome*. Society has been successful in labeling this problem a female issue and has done a poor job at unraveling why such a problem exists. But I believe we must take off the mask and discover the truth. Second, there is a certain level of confusion and unanswered questions surrounding outgrowing a mate. In many cases, although a woman feels she has outgrown her mate, her husband may still be a loving father, a committed family man and a hard worker. Even though there may be deep feelings of resentment, anguish and depression, for most women the idea of leaving their mates simply because they have outgrown them is not justification enough to walk away from relationships that seem solid in other areas.

Despite women's liberation and societal advances, women are not free of certain standards and responsibilities. Because of this, many women try to take on multiple roles: successful career woman, nurturing mother, attentive wife, budget-minded shopper and meal planner, gracious event planner and hostess and creative sexual partner. Let's not forget the personal and societal physical expectations of looking a certain way. Unfortunately these beliefs are not only held by society and the media, but also by women who continue to want to be all of those things.

Comparisons are everywhere in media and popular culture, from Martha Stewart to J.K. Rowlings. Constant exposure to successful female icons can negatively impact girls, often leading to anxiety, excessive dieting and compulsive/obsessive disorders.[1] The pressure on girls and women today to meet certain expectations is incredible and needs to stop. These expectations are fiction and do not accurately represent real life. I believe women need to ignore and break the superwoman fantasy. Many women are suffering from low self-esteem because they cannot meet the criteria that are supposed to make them successful women.

There is a belief that many women who suffer from the superwoman syndrome have low self-esteem. This belief is supported by the fact that many of them have problems with establishing boundaries and saying no to other people; they are constantly putting other people's needs before their own. It is imperative to mention that ladies who become "superwomen" because their husbands refuse to help around the house are another issue. A woman who becomes a superwoman because of imbalance in her marriage was usually not a superwoman before her relationship. She was effective, hardworking and productive, but maintained a sense of normalcy.

In fact, when a wife is forced to become both the husband and the wife in a marriage because she is accustomed to doing mostly everything in the household, her personal power and self-esteem are bolstered, not diminished. We will discuss this further in chapter 6.

Here are some questions women can ask themselves if they feel they may have outgrown their mates:

1. Am I often tired and exhausted from being overwhelmed with my life outside of my job?
2. Am I often filled with anger and resentment because my mate should be doing more to help around the house?
3. Is it easier to do the extra work myself than to take the time to teach my husband what to do?
4. Am I embarrassed by my husband because I feel others can very easily see the imbalance in our relationship?
5. On reflection, is my husband not very different from what he used to be before the marriage? Has he not grown much since we married?

6. Do I often resent how carefree and laidback my husband lives his life?
7. Am I physically disheveled and frumpy and in need of a makeover?
8. Are my thoughts scattered and I don't know what to do first?
9. Do I often compare myself to how my husband looks and realize that he appears more refreshing and youthful?
10. Has my physical appearance become less attractive and I don't have time to deal with how I look right now?
11. Has my desire for sex and intimacy drastically decreased and I find I want to be left alone?
12. Do I often wish my husband would take charge and help around the house without being asked?
13. Is my family starting to see me as a nag because I have to ask for help over and over again?
14. Do I often feel a sense of resentment and feel used or taken for granted by my husband?
15. Do the kids depend on me more than my husband, because they see me as the decision maker and the one who has the final word?
16. Does my husband tend to refrain from making simple decisions and ultimately feel more comfortable when I make the decisions for the household?

If you answered yes to eight or more of these questions, it is probable that you have an imbalance in your relationship and that you have outgrown your mate.

Living in the Same Household but Seeing Separately
Sandy knows that something is wrong. She feels drained physically and emotionally. She feels in a constant state of disgust. Though she tries to talk herself out of it, she feels like she is

being used, taken for granted and unappreciated. Often she is in a state of confusion, because some days she feels content and optimistic and other days she feels overwhelmed with numbness and sadness, wondering if life would be easier without her husband.

John and Sandy are both professional trainers for two large communication giants who celebrated their marriage with a large church wedding and have been married fifteen years. Both are longtime active members of their parish. They attend couples ministry outings and Bible study.

John often planned surprise romantic outings for Sandy when they were newlyweds. When he traveled on business, he left romantic notes at home for Sandy to find while he was away. John sent flowers on all special occasions—Valentine's Day, Sandy's birthday, Sweetie's Day and their anniversary.

Within two years of their marriage they were able to buy a five-bedroom home in a middle-class suburb. After settling in their new house, Sandy gave birth to their first child and then two years later a second child. Although motherhood required her to take time off, Sandy remained in her professional position. Her two maternity leaves prevented her from advancing to higher paying positions and she had to forego other advancements that would have required her to travel. Sandy undertook most of the responsibility of finding daycare for their two children. She has become the soccer mom, the dance lessons coordinator and the one to make sure the children are at choir rehearsal and summer day camp.

John, meanwhile, has become an avid golfer and enjoys sporting events, from college football to the professional teams. While John has been focused on his golf game, Sandy has been focused on the kids' extracurricular activities and social development. John is financially planning for their children's college educations while Sandy wonders if she should go back to school and pursue a master's degree, because advancement within her company is very limited. The two rarely have time alone, because they are so busy doing other things. On the surface they appear to be a happy and successful couple. Deep down, however, Sandy feels like a single parent in need of a new mate who will share in the concerns and obligation of the family while John feels that life is fine and there are no major concerns.

Sandy understands that John is a good man. She feels that compared to her girlfriends' bad relationships John would definitely be worth keeping in most women's eyes. In fact, she knows that he would not be single long if they were to separate. He treats her with love and respect. There have never been any signs of infidelity. He is a committed family man and a great father: There is no question of his devotion and love for his family.

However, due to Sandy's level of stress she wonders if he is enough for her. She has begun to wonder if they are still compatible socially, spiritually and emotionally. Sandy feels that she has been forced to grow and mature very quickly due to the stress in her professional career and family life. John, on the other hand, may have grown in some ways but because his life is more carefree, there has not been as much of a need to change and mature. He did not have the same sense of urgency to grow up, because Sandy feels she did all of the maturing for him. Sandy took on most of the responsibility, so therefore she changed the most.

She feels guilty for thinking this way, but this same thought keeps haunting her day and night: She can't help but wonder if possibly through the years she has outgrown John. If it is true, is there still any future hope for a happy and balanced relationship? She is starting to feel shamefully embarrassed by him because she is sure that people who know them have also noticed that she has grown and matured while he has comfortably stayed the same. It is obvious not only through their personalities and the topics that come up for discussion, but also in how they look physically. John looks fabulous, fit and happy while Sandy has gained twenty-five pounds and is in desperate need of a makeover. Sandy is sure that John is also uncomfortable around her family. She finds him laughing inappropriately at conversations that are not funny and wanting to leave early at family functions. She wonders if her imagination of what people must be saying is worse than what is actually being whispered, but it still hurts to think that people are talking at all. *The imbalance in their relationship became clear one day when she found her husband playing video games in the bedroom while she was looking for a second job in the help wanted section of Sunday's newspaper.*

As a life coach, I feel strongly that this is a rising problem facing couples today. *Unfortunately, many wives believe that they can change their husbands once they get married and oftentimes their husbands have no clue that there is any need to change. Relationships become difficult because of what wives know and what husbands don't know.* Today this kind of imbalance in a marriage is most obvious in three specific areas: financially, emotionally and spiritually.

Historically, we have been taught that men have the sole responsibility to support and take care of their families. Although things are changing, any reality outside this structure tends to look odd, strange and inappropriate to the common relationship today. However, the workforce to which we have been accustomed is changing and it is certainly becoming more and more common for women to earn more money annually than their husbands. According to the Bureau of Labor Statistics, in 1987 only 17.8 percent of women made more money than their husbands, but in 2007, 25.9 percent made more.[2]

The stress and reality of such women's lives have pushed females to equip themselves quicker and invest in more education and other areas of personal development. When the difference in salary is drastically higher than their husbands', it is common for women to feel like they have too much responsibility and their positions in their families are wrong. We will discuss this in more detail in chapter 3.

Measuring His Value

Is his value measured by his bank account or the time he spends at home? This question begins with the stereotypes and past practices of our society. Only thirty years ago, some women started feeling more comfortable leaving their children every day to work outside the home when their families needed two incomes. Traditionally it has been the childhood dream of most women to have picture perfect weddings and marry tall, dark and handsome men who would love and provide for them and their beautiful children the rest of their lives. And, if the women did decide to work outside the home they would, at least, have the option to stay at home. Under the mask of societal standing and a fancy degree, there is still, for some, the desire not to have to work every day, but instead to have a choice. Some women, even today, believe the ideal life is having a husband who is able to provide for the family, with the wife's income being the extra money. For some women there is a hidden and unspoken belief that the measure of a man's love is how much money he is willing to spend on his wife. Traditionally, this has represented ultimately how much he loved his wife—*the bigger his love the deeper his pocket some people believed*.

However, the modern day standard of love has changed drastically. Now a woman is more likely to also value the strength of her marriage on how much time her husband spends with her or how willing he is to help with household chores. Although women's perspectives on love have changed, society's views of men have not. The success of a man is still measured by the worth of his possessions and the depth of his bank account.

The reality is that what many wives really desire is for their mates to have the financial worth of the past standards with the skills of a stay-at-home dad. This becomes much more of an issue when the wife is making more money than her mate in addition to carrying the majority of the responsibilities at home. When this happens, it becomes less and less obvious why she is staying with her husband.

Another common problem women often mention to me is that when they do bring enough income home to pay the bills and support the family, some men feel that their own paychecks should be kept for their own personal pleasures or building financial worth. It has become a rising occurrence with men who know that their wives' incomes can carry the bills and the responsibilities of the family to completely dismiss their financial responsibilities to the household. Unless this problem is rectified, it is nearly impossible for the couple to maintain a meaningful relationship. Unfortunately, in this type of man's eyes, a wife is seen as being a constant nag and complainer about the imbalance and unhappiness in her life; she sees her husband as an extra weight that is simply coming along for the ride.

Emotional deprivation seems to be the one sentiment that occurs when there is any imbalance at all. Whether it stems from social, financial or emotional differences, research has found that if imbalance is found in these areas it can affect women emotionally. This can cause women to feel that they are no longer compatible with their husbands. They feel as if their perspectives about what is important in life have moved and grown beyond their husbands'. The perspectives from which they question life's meaning and make decisions are deeper and more mature. For example, instead of buying a two-door sports car because it makes her feel good, a woman may settle for a low mileage four-door van so there is enough room when it is her turn to carpool the neighborhood children. In time, she learns to love the van she once disliked because of how practical it has become for her family. When women can't relate to their mates emotionally it is difficult having any type of relationship with them. It is hard for wives to bring up dreams and visions for the future, because they question whether their mates will sacrifice and do what it takes to make the dreams reality. Women find that they have to continually explain what they mean and so they don't enjoy conversations and dialogues with the men they once loved deeply.

Often, women's individual faiths tend to be one of the most important areas in their lives. For a woman who has strong faith, it becomes very important that she find someone with whom to share her beliefs. Someone who can relate to the core and the essence for why she does what she does. In many cases, one's faith is the basis for every major decision and change in life. It affects a woman's friends, her energy level and the overall perspective of how she lives her life. Practicing a faith makes a woman feel more fulfilled, because she begins to feel peace and security in areas about which her husband complains. This can begin to affect the communication barrier in the relationship because she stops discussing with him her personal and professional concerns. However, many women feel that even if they can't share their spiritual journeys with their significant others, if their husbands would assist in making life livable by being committed and active in other areas, it would be worth the tradeoff. Many women seem to be willing to compromise and accept the spiritual imbalance.

Because, as we discussed, the man of today is still very much measured by both his bank account and the time that he spends at home, these two contrasting areas make it very difficult for any man to completely fulfill the expectations of his wife and the opinions of others. When a person makes an abundant amount of money it usually increases the demand for more hours and focus on his career. A person in this position usually does not have time to help with dinner and laundry at night. But if a husband takes the time to help the children with homework in the evenings, it makes it more difficult to meet the expectations of a high-powered job. *The expectations that women have of their mates oftentimes are not very realistic or fair and are often expectations that they would not be able to accomplish themselves.* The time spent at home with the family has increased in value due to the ability of women to make more money for the household. Making more money often means less time at home, which in turn increases her individual stress.

The depth of the man's bank account has and will always be the biggest area measuring his value to his family and the world. There will always be a belief that the more money a man makes the more of a catch he is. This belief is shared by many women, society and also many men themselves. Men will often measure their self-worth on what they do, how much money they have and the level of power they have achieved. It is a powerful ego boost to be too busy and important to have the time to wash the dishes. As the stress of life for women increases, the need to have men with more domestic abilities and willingness also increases.

Let's look at the top relationship problems that tend to surface when women have outgrown their mates. These are also the major issues for divorce today.

♦ **Lack of relationship commitment**
   Lack of commitment continues to be a top reason why marriages don't last. Because marriage doesn't always

happen out of true love or friendship, one partner may lack commitment. People marry for various reasons. It could be to increase their images, to be more secure financially or due to a lack of direction in their own lives. The unhappier a woman is in a relationship, the less sex and intimacy in the marriage and the likelier a woman is to seek companionship outside of the relationship. Something to think about: Many experts believe that spouses don't cheat if they have married their best friends.

♦ **Lack of communication**
Without communication, relationships are doomed. Keeping resentments to oneself is not only unhealthy, but also unfair to a mate. It is not a partner's responsibility to ascertain why a mate is upset. The more resentment a woman has, the more angry she will become. Angry communication will produce distance but not results. When husbands feel they are constantly getting yelled at they have the tendency to shut down and stop all pertinent communication.

♦ **Inability to manage conflict**
A lack of maturity or a lack of concern for the other person inhibits one partner's ability to manage conflicts and handle irreconcilable differences. The inability to resolve conflict results in long-term resentment and may eventually destroy the relationship. When there is imbalance, wives tend to become angry, frustrated and nagging and many times husbands will stop talking completely.

♦ **Different goals**
In some marriages, one partner feels the need and the financial obligation to move forward and progress while the other spouse is perfectly happy. This can cause resentment at the point when one partner feels that she is contributing more than the other.

◆ **Different expectations**
When partners have different expectations for their relationships, finances and day-to-day living, relationships are
affected drastically. One spouse feels stressed and like she
is doing too much while the other spouse is still wondering what needs to be done. Financial strain exacerbates
this problem "because material needs remain unfulfilled
and creates discontent in the minds of both the partners." The partner making the most money and the one
who is the most motivated will likely feel that the other
partner is less able-bodied.

◆ **Intellectual incompatibility**
Misunderstandings are in many cases the result of
intellectual incompatibility. The mate who feels smarter
usually develops a sense of arrogance and becomes unfair
and judgmental toward the other mate.

◆ **Lifestyle differences**
When lifestyle differences, including culture and religion,
clash, it creates a marital atmosphere that is very difficult
for people who are passionate about their beliefs and
habits. When a partner feels his or her beliefs or practices
are threatened, he or she is not usually open to giving in.[3]

Is it Love or is it Sympathy?

Janice and Henry married after only a year-long courtship. They
both earned their law degrees from the same university. Janice
works for a private law firm and Henry works for a state agency.
They have two children and share in parenting responsibilities.
Janice earns more than Henry in private practice and has been
happy with the progress of her career. She volunteers on two
local bar committees and enjoys participating in the school PTA.

Henry finds his job frustrating and his pay equally unsatis-
fying. He constantly complains to Janice about his lack of
autonomy at work, but he does little to correct the situation

with his supervisor or colleagues. In spite of his dissatisfaction with his job, he does not quit in order to provide security for his family. His willingness to accept things without challenge or question tends to translate into his marriage as well. Recently, Janice wanted to invest more money in riskier hedge funds while Henry wanted to stay with their standard mutual funds that provide only modest returns on their investment. When Janice wanted to refinance their home mortgage loan from their higher fixed rate to a lower adjustable rate, Henry balked at the idea. He was worried that if rates rose unexpectedly they might not be able to refinance again, especially if one of them unexpectedly lost his or her job. Henry's conservatism and fear of change leaves Janice feeling vulnerable. She longs for a mate whose strength and courage would enhance her willingness to take risks and encourage their children to do the same. Yet, she knows that Henry is a good man who loves his family.

At the beginning this couple seemed balanced. There were areas where Janice was obviously stronger, but Henry balanced her just as generously. He had a calming effect that added a soft touch, which was just what Janice needed. The balance with the discipline of the children was incredible: Janice's style was like a piece of steel, but Henry was more like soft red velvet lying over the steel.

As life became more complex, Janice started needing more from Henry. His calming effect is nice sometimes, but when it comes to real life situations she needs his calmness to turn to strength and focus. She needs his patience to turn into realistic expectations and action. Henry's parental guidance with the kids remains the exact same way, exhibiting no change from when they were three-year-old toddlers to thirteen-year-old teenagers. Janice wants his loving discipline with the children to become a strong adult versus child relationship that can map the directions for their futures. After some life challenges, she realizes what at one time brought balance to her life actually started being a roadblock for her family and personal growth. Henry's unending calmness and patience appears to her more like a cowardly way out than a man with substance and authority.

As much as she hates to admit it, when Janice considers the possibility of leaving Henry, she is surprised to realize that the main reason she is still committed to her marriage is because she feels sorry for Henry and wants to protect him from the cruelty of real life. She often wonders how his next wife would treat him. Janice does not feel that Henry has good sense at all. He is a smart man and a successful attorney and she knows that he accomplished all that on his own. But his lack of life motivation worries her. His unwillingness to question people and circumstances and his compliance to accept life and challenges at status quo make Janice view Henry as unprepared and ill equipped to face the world without her. She loves him but she questions if she is really "in love" with him. She often says to herself that if he just was not such a good guy and a wonderful person she would not sympathize with him so deeply. He is like a grown-up boy who simply has no clue.

Janice starts to question if she ever truly loved Henry or if the strong emotion she continues to have toward him is simply a love for his personhood interspersed sympathy for his manhood. She starts to wonder if she made a mistake and confused sympathy with love.

It is important to recognize that you can love a person without being "in love" with a person. Many people actually don't know the difference between the two. I often counsel that if you have to question whether you are "in love" with a person it is best to assume that you are not. *When you are "in love" you know it and you will not have to question.*

Let's explore a few different types of love:

♦ *Companionate* love is not sexual, intimate or based on any particular bond. For example, you can love a stranger

walking down the street whom you have never met
before. The type of love that most people prematurely
seek and often become confused about is *passionate* love.
In contrast to companionate love, passionate love
involves "infatuation, intense preoccupation with the
partner, strong sexual longing, throes of ecstasy and feelings of exhilaration" from being with the partner.[4]

♦ *Eros* love focuses on the self, *philia* love is that of a
friendship, *physio* love relates to the brain's sex drive and
eroticism and *agape* love is self-sacrificing love.[5]

♦ *Platonic* love, as most people know it, is a love relationship without a sexual connection or desire. Many people
experience deep friendships that are non-sexual, a good
example of platonic love. This conventional view is
actually a misinterpretation of platonic love ideal, which
is "based not on lack of erotic interest but on spiritual
transmutation of the sex force, opening up vast expanses
of subtler enjoyments than sex."[6]

♦ *Storgic* love is also called *familial* love and has a few
different interpretations. Derived from the Greek word
for natural affection, storgic love can apply to a parent's
love for her child, the love between two close friends and
the sexual relationship of two partners that developed
from their friendship. In this last example of storgic love,
the partners are friends first and have a high level of commitment. While storgic lovers have a strong "level of
friendship, understanding, and intimacy...disadvantages
may include a lack of passion and potential boredom in
the relationship."[7]

One key element to truly giving of yourself in any type of
love relationship is you must first love yourself before you can
be free enough to love anyone else. Many people are quick to

call their relationships love because of personal voids within themselves. They know that they are missing something, yet they neglect to look at themselves first. Women who love themselves first have the ability to love without needing and can relate to their mates without smothering them. When women are in love relationships and have not grown an appreciation and respect for themselves first, they become needy, desperate and anxious in their relationships. They have feelings of insecurity and self-doubt instead of feelings of love and assurance. The neediness and uncertainty becomes unfair to partners because they have to deal with companions who are incomplete. Needy people expect their partners to be everything to them and to do everything for them. Oftentimes, needy people want partners to decrease their friendships with other people, because needy people want to be around their partners constantly and they feel insecure and paranoid about their partners' relationships with others. A needy partner develops a relationship into one that breeds resentment and disharmony, because he or she is not mentally or emotionally prepared to love someone else.

Many times, when a couple starts developing a relationship, it is easy for partners to believe that as long as they are feeling "something" and it is not negative, then it must be love. This belief could not be further from the truth. People call it love because they are often looking for love; many people spend their time seeking love. Other emotions that can be confused with love are admiration, curiosity, a strong liking for the other person and sympathy. However, love is often the only emotion we consider when feelings develop.

At the beginning of a relationship, when you can clearly see your mate as someone who is either equal or similar to you in the areas of intelligence, energy level and success, it is more likely that when positive feelings rise, you are feeling a strong liking that will gradually develop into love.

On the other hand, at the beginning of the relationship it is obvious that you are the one with the most vision, direction and personal success. Hence, it is very likely that sympathy is a strong part of what you feel for the other person, which in a long-term relationship often develops into resentment.

Is it Love or is it Need?

Bob knew that his relationship with Sarita was unbalanced from the beginning. He did not take this too seriously, because he and Sarita were both so young when they started dating. He had no idea they would actually commit to a lifetime relationship and get married.

It seemed that the materialistic pleasures of life came to Sarita first. Yes, Bob wished that he had a car first, but he did not have two parents who could supply the down payment for a vehicle. It would have been nice for him to further his education and finish college, too, but no one told him about the grants he could possibly get to continue his schooling. Sarita's luck in life seemed to continue until she greatly exceeded where Bob was. Her college degree allowed her to get a better job. Due to her career opportunities, it allowed them to get a brand new home. Although her first car was old with a lot of miles, by the time she got her second car, in her early twenties, she was able to get a brand new one from the dealership.

Sometimes it was hard for Bob to feel like Sarita was the reason for most of their success, because he felt just as successful as her. Because they shared everything as a couple, her good fortune also became his. Her car became their car. Once they were married, her home was equally shared by him. They did not believe in separate bank accounts. Their money was combined, so it was hard to tell who had contributed what. This joint venture flowed over into their personal life as well. When other people saw them together, they saw them as a successful couple. They were not viewed as separate people and no one wondered who the first one was to make certain achievements.

Later in their marriage, it was obvious that they had little in common and that Sarita had become disgruntled with Bob's overall contribution. Sarita often brought up the subject of divorce but Bob did whatever he could to patch things up, because his life was much more privileged with her than without her.

Bob and Sarita's situation provides a good example of a classic marriage that suffers from extreme economic imbalance. Even before Sarita married Bob, she realized that there was an economical imbalance. But, like many people she was in a rush to get married and assumed that things would one day change for the better. She did not understand that if this was an area that she was uncomfortable with before the marriage, she should have assumed that the same pattern would continue throughout the marriage. Too often, people, especially women, assume that relationship problems will change for the better after they say "I do"; but in reality, the opposite usually happens. *If there is a problem before the marriage, it usually elevates a few degrees higher after the marriage.* One very important issue that women often never consider is the impact this imbalance has on their partners. More often than not, most couples try to ignore the existence of this problem. When this happens, it allows for negative internal feelings to brew and for long-term resentment to set in, especially in women. Although men may never bring up the reality of imbalances, they may instead feel useless or as though they can't do anything right. They may also have a lack of purpose and meaning along with a strong awareness that they are not needed and that their partners can do everything themselves.

Unlike many relationship problems, this one has the power to destroy a relationship forever. Because, as we have discussed, the value of a man in terms of power and economical advantage directly affects his personal ego, confidence level and the way that society views him. To admit failure or a lack of power in this area is one of the most difficult things for a man to do. He knows that due to his economic disadvantage, he has less power and therefore is at more of a risk for a lonely and financially broke future. Many men in this position choose to ignore the problem and enjoy the advantages that the relationship brings.

A true and healthy love stands alone without the emotion of need. *True love is when you are not with the person because you need to be, but because you want to be.* Being with someone on the basis of need establishes desperateness and a false sense of self for the one who is in need. Lack of respect and an overwhelming sense of authority and control can easily take over the mindset of the other partner. When the spouse who is needy can balance what he or she doesn't have monetarily with what he or she can give domestically, the balance of the relationship can be saved and possibly healed. Today many women are trying to communicate to their husbands, "I make good money, so I don't need money from you; but what I do need is for you to support my goals, be a partner raising the kids and a faithful friend and companion." Those attributes are growing in popularity and sometimes are exceeding the need for monetary balance.

Is it the Mother's Fault?

Now let us raise and answer two major questions as to why the idea of outgrowing a mate is such a major issue in many relationships. The questions that will be explored are 1) Is it partially the man's mother's fault there are so many imbalances in his family? 2) Could the tendency toward naivety of the male have inhibited him from growing into the person his wife needs?

Mama's Boys

Although every man who was loved instead of taught does not become a "mama's boy" there are a large number who do. Why do many women have an automatic dislike for "mama's boys"?

Women always like hearing a potential mate speak about his mother in caring and respectful manners. In fact, men who have good relationships with their mothers tend to be more understanding and respectful toward women and women are aware of this. However, a man who talks too much about his mother will raise a "mama's boy" flag in the minds of many women. Let's explore a little further why many women don't like mama's boys.

Just as young men often fantasize about sexy nurses or French maids, young women often fantasize about firemen and policemen, who represent men who display strength, power and masculinity. If a sexy fireman had to check with his mother every time he took off his clothes for a girl, his sex appeal would definitely fade. Women generally like strong men who aren't intimidated or easily influenced by other people. That's one of the main reasons why women don't like mama's boys.

Mama's boys often fulfill their mothers' every wish, especially the most unreasonable ones—and that's where the problems start. If a man carries out his mother's every request, chances are that he will not make decisions with his significant other without his mother's approval. It's hard enough to share decisions as a couple, so it is rare that a woman will tolerate a third person interfering in her relationship with her husband. When a girl is twelve and her boyfriend can't go out because his mother doesn't approve, it's okay because he's still a child. When that boy becomes a man and his mother still rules his life, there is a problem with both the man and his mother. The man has a problem, because he is still looking to his mother for guidance. He has not properly separated himself. This could be a sign of low self-esteem and fear of his mother's rejection. Many times this issue occurs in a man who is incomplete and truly not ready for an intimate relationship. Often men are pressured to please their mothers and they are looking for constant approval just like they were when they were children.

When a mother supports this dependent behavior from her son, it also suggests that she needs to move on with her life and that the love she has for her son is not healthy. If a mother's love is healthy, she wants her son to develop long, loving and authentic relationships with other people. This occurs when the mother can trust her son enough to make sound and practical decisions for himself. The same unhealthy dependence that the son has with his mother is the same dependence that the mother has with the son. However, it is usually the mother who fuels, expects and keeps the dependency going. She is the one who has the power to release the guilt and she also has the power to let her son go gently and free him to live the life in which hopefully she has prepared him to succeed.

If a woman shares a man's bed, she probably won't settle for being in second position in his life. It is normal and expected that a man will give his mother special attention on her birthday, Mother's Day or other celebrations. However, if a man always puts his mother before his wife, no matter what the occasion, chances are his wife will end up resenting both him and his mother. Another major reason why women don't like mama's boys is because competing with the woman who gave birth to her husband is a fight the wife feels she simply can't win. *If the mother-in-law is in the picture too much, it can make a woman feel like she isn't doing a good job keeping her husband happy since he still has another woman in his life.* Women like to know they're making their mates happy. They don't want to hear that they can't do things as well as their mates' mothers.

Men sometimes make the mistake of telling their mothers private matters. Often, women expect men to have difficulties talking about intimate issues, so when a woman finds out her husband has been speaking to his mother about their problems, she feels betrayed, embarrassed and violated. I recently heard about Jill, a wife who received a gift certificate for a fine lingerie store from her mother-in-law. She thought it was a thoughtful gesture until her mother-in-law added, "And don't buy plain cotton underwear. Josh just doesn't like them." Jill felt humiliated that her husband had shared such intimate details about her with his mother and hurt that he was unable to communicate his preference directly to her.

Fortunately, if you have a husband who has been cursed with the mama's boy syndrome, there are ways he can show equal love and respect to both you and his mother. The first thing a man can do to avoid being a mama's boy is *create a new relationship with his mother as an adult*. Yes, his relationship with his mother should be distinctively different from when he was a child versus when he is grown. If he has been called a mama's boy, chances are his mother is too intrusive and he needs to learn how to say "no" to her. She might be saintly, but it doesn't mean that she isn't needy, unreasonable and manipulative. *His mother already knows her son loves his wife and would do anything for her and that is precisely the problem.* So, once in a while, despite her tears and attempts at *emotional blackmail*, he needs to let his mother know how good his wife is to him and that she is the priority in his life.

It is important a wife lets her husband continue to share with his mother, so he can tell his mother that he is looking forward to the romantic weekend he has planned for himself and his wife. It is also okay to tell his mother that she doesn't need to make sandwiches for the road and that his wife is making sandwiches instead. Speaking up to his mother will change the entire scope of his life. It will increase his personal self-confidence, it will add to the respect and love his wife has for the mother-in-law and it will develop boldness in him that he will need not only personally, but professionally as well.

Loving Versus Teaching

Many of us have heard the saying *mothers have the tendency to love their boys but teach their girls*. It has been a common thread through traditional child rearing to protect and shelter the male. Unlike other practices, this tendency has crossed all cultural boundaries. It is not partial to ethnicity or race. It is a practice that has plagued most homes, without mothers or children being fully aware of it. It is not uncommon for fathers to consistently mention to their wives, "Stop babying him; he is not going to be successful in life; you are ruining him." It is common for fathers to become aware of the favoritism that they see in their families, but they are also ignorant of the seriousness of the problem and the lasting and profound effect that this favoritism will have.

Most mothers are shocked at the suggestion that they rear their sons differently than their daughters. In many cases it seems to come natural for mothers to want to nurture sons with a softer and more lenient hand, regardless of their ages. Most daughters feel the difference in how their brothers are raised while growing up. Eventually many realize that they were required to do more chores around the house, that they were talked to with a sterner style and a clearer direction of right and wrong and that they were given stricter discipline. It is also common for daughters to have earlier curfews than their brothers and for their friends to be screened more critically. *Although in many cases daughters are deeply loved by their mothers, it is a different type of love—a love that makes teaching as important as loving.* As soon as a daughter is born, it is understood she must be directed in a path of responsibility and accountability.

Some experts suggest that the same sex parent has the most influence on children. This means that fathers have the most influence on sons and mothers have the most influence on daughters. In many cases, the softer attitude toward daughters comes from fathers. When the father is present in the home, he tends to raise his daughter with the same tendencies that the mother has with their son. Although the father has influence over a daughter, the power of the influence is very different from the mother's. His softer attitude does not result in a dependent, directionless and needy daughter. Usually it has no negative influence on her ability to be responsible and motivated, although it often can influence what she expects and wants from her future mate. Let's discover why the father's influence is often not as influential as the mother's.

In too many cases, the father is not actually in the home. The number of single parent households is increasing. According to the U.S. Census Bureau, there are 9.9 million mother-only households.[1] When the father is not consistently around, he has less power and therefore harbors a minor influence on his children and his family in general.

Because most fathers are also grown men who were loved and not taught, they are unaware and unconditioned on how to teach their children to be responsible. When a father finds the need to try to teach, oftentimes his style is often either too soft or too harsh to have the type of influence that is needed. Because women tend to be more intense, passionate and full of unconditional love, the influence of the mother is very strong; she traditionally rules and sets the tone for the entire household.

This mindset that mothers love their sons and teach their daughters affects their future relationships. Women, in general, tend not to expect as much from men as they do from themselves, because they have been taught that they can accomplish more at one time. This was clear when they watched their mothers raise their brothers. Unfortunately, most women are also taught early in life that having a quality relationship with a man brings ultimate satisfaction and completeness and that no other relationship in life equates to the same level of love and commitment. It is many women's ultimate goal in life to be swept off their feet and be loved forever. *Then their husbands who were loved but not taught become men who are loved but not taught.* This outgrowth between genders usually happens when the children are very young. It is not uncommon for a four-year-old sister to have more maturity, focus and confidence than her seven-year-old brother. Although it would be unfair to say that the mother is solely to blame, it is only fair to mention that her distinction between raising her daughter and son does play a significant role in why women tend to outgrow men.

The reality is that many women learn to settle in a relationship, because they are afraid to be alone. When one's aim in life is to become a wife and mother, it is easy for a sense of desperateness to overshadow smart and practical decisions. Although women can sense imbalances, even as early as the dating stage, because they are trying to win men's love and affection they are careful not to nag or bother men in fear that the men may lose interest in them. As we learned in chapter 1, even in today's modern thinking many women equate the quality of their lives by the measure and depth of love their husbands have for them. *In many cases, a woman's goal is marriage and a man's goal is power.*

Women feel it is necessary to create environments that men enjoy so they won't want to leave and will always be there with them. This compromise of putting men first, above a woman's own personal needs, starts in the teenage dating years. When this boyfriend turns into her husband and he starts getting involved in a *real* marriage relationship, he will often have to be taught by his wife some of the principles he never received from his parents. It is common for him to be resentful, because he does not want his wife to teach him the basics. Her doing so makes him feel like less than a man and more like a child.

The wife also has a sense of resentment, because she expected her husband to be more responsible than what he actually is. His lack of certain basics simply causes more stress and doubt in her life. She is also overwhelmed with the fact that she has to now become a teacher to someone who resents being taught.

It is common for the husband to have to learn the principles of spending, because he did not have to be accountable to anyone for how he spent his money in the past. In some cases he just asked his mother for the money he needed and she rushed to give it to him with no expectations of being paid back. While his wife is trying to give him a course in "Spending Principles 101", the bills still have to be paid and the money still needs to be budgeted. She quickly finds that it is easier to just do it herself than to teach the principles step-by-step to her husband.

Today, men's lack of knowledge tends to be most prevalent in areas of finance, family planning, career decisions and personal responsibility. These are the four areas that bring women the most frustration. Most women find that it is easier to be both the man and the woman and just do everything themselvesinstead of schooling their husbands on "How to Keep Your Wife Happy 101."

"Do everything yourself" is the theme that travels through many two-person households. Although this appears to be a quick fix for right now, it is disastrous for the long-term. If the quick fix is done by the wife, she starts feeling frustrated and disappointed that she does not have more help and support from her husband. It appears to her that he simply takes for granted the extras that she does and he doesn't realize or appreciate the luxury of having everything done for him. *In many cases, she finds that he truly believes that anything outside of going to work and then coming home is an extra duty. Her frustration turns into anger and then eventually her anger turns into long-term resentment.* Although these feelings result in her being explosive at times, she still continues to do everything for everyone, because she has now become a pro at it. Meanwhile, the husband does not understand her burst of anger and frustration that seems to come more and more frequently in their marriage. He tries to understand, but really doesn't quite believe that she needs more help around the house when she seems to handle everything so perfectly herself.

Because of this sudden outburst and the consistent complaining that is so common in their marriage, he starts labeling her as a constant nag who is stressed out, unhappy and ungrateful. He continues to be the calm and disciplined one who never quite understands the source of her anger or what the fuss is all about. At times she feels inadequate, fool-hearted and mean-spirited because, compared to her husband, she is the one always complaining about what needs to change. She agrees that she does not like what she has become.

It would be easier for him to understand his wife's anger if he did not overhear his father, brothers and male friends also trying to figure out why their wives have become so sour, resentful and unhappy. He just assumes that it must be a "female" thing.

Nice Guys and Naivety

Sex, as it relates to the "nice guy", has been a main focus for many experts. Some experts suggest women only claim to seek a nice guy while other women actually want a nice guy. Conventional wisdom maintains that women prefer sensitive men, perpetuating the nice guy theory.

Nice guys don't have the best reputation, however. Even though nice guys are stronger companions in long-term, committed relationships, many view nice guys as soft, weak, emasculated and asexual. This is because many nice guys feel they must hide their sexual desires. Many women feel the need to be with men who are powerful and strongly sexual, so many women wind up with guys who are not nice. A nice guy may have these alluring characteristics, but because he hides them, women may overlook him.[2]

Many parents tell you that, more often than not, baby girls act as though they have been in the world before and baby boys are sweet, loveable and curious about life. *This difference in confidence and personality begins when children are very young. Then parents raise children based on how they act instead of how they should act.* Instead of enhancing what children need in their personalities for balance, adventure and responsibility, parents tend to take what is given without any questions.

A personality imbalance can destroy a relationship. Sometimes a mate can be just "too nice" for the relationship to mature. Instead of being smart, one partner is nice and instead of making the best long-term decisions he or she is too worried about the opinion of others. Because a successful relationship requires maturity, responsibility and deep perspective, being "too nice" can become a roadblock for the union to grow.

The nice guy syndrome usually affects men when they are young. Many times women desire nice guys to be a little more risky, daring and mysterious. Often, women find that they are actually more attracted to guys who are not so nice. Because of Joe's natural calming and genuine personality, he is a little less desirable than Tom the motorcycle man, who wears that black leather jacket every chance he gets. The nice guy's heart is kind, his perspective is pure and innocent, his past is clean and he is, without a doubt, decent. He really is the type of man to take home to Mother. The nice guy personality type gives women hope that there really are good men in the world. Worrying about being embarrassed by his unacceptable language in the company of others would never be a concern. The nice guy is a smart choice: an ideal father who would do anything in the world for his mate. He accepts his spouse as she is. But, as good as it may seem, there is something about knowing that he would do "anything in the world for you" that causes a woman to question her satisfaction with him.

As a woman's life matures and becomes more complex, she notices that her nice guy husband's unending loyalty and commitment does not 100 percent satisfy her and that something is definitely missing. She starts needing more from him in a different way. She finds herself thinking, "If he only had more aspirations and a backbone or if he just did not play it so darn safe all the time, then he would be the perfect guy."

It is possible for a man to be nice and still be a risk taker and mysterious, but it is rare. Being nice to the extent that a man is labeled "a nice guy" often means that the man is so nice that he has a problem saying no and has the tendency to put other people's needs above his own. Some claim that a nice guy can be seen a mile away. His niceness is displayed in the way he walks, talks and even the way he moves his head. Unlike other guys, many genuine nice guys never learn to be "street smart" as society expects them to be, because they tend to battle with over trusting. Often, because a woman tends to be smitten quickly with his nice personality, she is fast to make an exception about other physical and character attributes. But once she gets accustomed to his nice tendencies, it does not take long for her to start getting in touch with her real feelings about what she wants and desires in her mate. She feels guilty, because she knows that her wishes for a tougher persona are shallow and that they do not reflect his personal character or integrity. Deep down she knows that it would never justify a breakup or a temporary separation, but as hard as she tries for it not to make a difference, it does. In every touch, each time they kiss, as he reaches to be more intimate, as hard as she tries not to care about the differences between her vision of a more multifaceted partner and his niceness—she does.

Unless a woman has been in a mentally or physically abusive relationship, sometimes it is hard to fully appreciate the abilities of the nice guy. She might think she is different from other women who seek bad boys, but she quickly learns that she has the same curiosity about guys who are not "nice guys." With a nice guy, she finds herself not quite as smitten or giving 100 percent to the relationship as she wishes. She sometimes starts to wonder if she is really "in love" with her nice guy.

As he continues to be nice, she finds herself changing. She remembers when she was "nice" as well and when it used to be hard to say no. *She finds her personality changing from nice to pleasant, from pleasant to fair.* She does not mean to change so drastically but past life experiences and responsibilities force her to think quicker, deeper and more analytically.

When a man's main and most dominant characteristic is *niceness*, we see that it can too often be a tradeoff for other things such as passion and confidence that are just as important in a fulfilling relationship. It is imperative to know that when considering a long-term partner in "the nice husband", and this is all that he has going for him, it is usually not enough to keep the interest of a maturing wife.

3

Financial and Infidelity Stressors

Financial Issues

For most people in committed relationships, finances, according to experts, have been the number one relationship destroyer. The lack of and the struggle with having enough money has been a constant stressor that many relationships have not been able to endure and overcome. How the money is being used, where the money is going and the need for more money are issues that must be addressed in long-term relationships. Whenever two people share the same household and combine their earnings, even in just the smallest way, this can initiate loud arguments and cause tension between the partners. Money has significant emotional power and influence. Since couples have to use money in order to survive, at least on some level, it is a relationship matter that will always have to be handled regardless of how rich or poor a person is.

Both partners have separate, hurtful areas. The source of anger in the female often comes down to who carries the load and the responsibility for paying the bills. Now, she may still want him to help with bathing the children at night or washing the dishes after dinner; but, for the most part, many women would much prefer for their husbands to be out making money and providing for the family. *Some ladies feel they have outgrown their mates when they are doing a lot more than their spouses and their spouses have no intentions of catching up or making up the difference somewhere else in their relationships.* The problem begins when a husband comes home, sits on the couch and watches television programs all evening when there are obvious chores to do and his wife must do them. In fact, there is an unspoken expectancy for the woman to carry the load in the household when the husband's main responsibility is paying the bills and providing for the family. Even if the wife works too, usually the more money her husband brings in the less complaining she does. In this situation there is more understanding when both roles have been sufficiently defined. Unfortunately there often are arguments that grow more heated as time passes if there is imbalance not only in this crucial area, but also in other parts of the relationship. However, the financial disputes carry the most weight if unresolved.

It Will Never Work if He Can't Accept Himself

Maria married Mark when she was twenty-five years old. Mark works steadily as an automobile mechanic and Maria is a registered nurse. Although she knows that Mark's self-esteem could stand to be higher, Maria also knows that he is a good husband and a loyal person. Oftentimes Maria feels concerned about moving ahead and fulfilling her dreams, because she can tell that Mark is uncomfortable with her when she accomplishes her professional goals. She really wants to pursue a master's degree, but fears that it will destroy her relationship with Mark.

Maria is confused, because Mark often brings up the fact that she has a degree and he doesn't. He compares his salary to hers and recently has started accusing Maria of thinking that she is better than him. Although sometimes Mark wonders if he is being a little unfair, he doesn't understand why Maria has changed so much since their marriage. Neither one of them had a degree before the marriage and Mark doesn't understand why Maria seems to have become so much of a snob or why she has to get a degree. Maria keeps assuring him that she is fine with his job as long as he works and brings in a consistent paycheck, but Mark refuses to believe that she can ever be really happy with him in the long-term. Maria feels stuck, falsely accused and unhappy, while Mark feels embarrassed and uncomfortable because of Maria's success.

In 2006, 26 percent of wives earned more than their husbands.[1] Although everyone is becoming more used to the idea of women carrying the financial load, we are still a long way from true acceptance and non-judgment when it comes to this non-traditional lifestyle.

There are four levels of understanding that are imperative for married couples to understand when a woman has outgrown a man financially and he has low self-esteem:

1. It is first very important that a woman is sure she is absolutely comfortable with her husband even if he never pursues a degree in the future and if she continues to make more money than he makes. She needs to consider the worst-case scenario, search her soul and see if she can love him without resentment and without secretly hoping that he was a more motivated, career-focused mate.

    There are some important questions you need to ask yourself and deeply reflect on because they will determine if you should remain in relationship like this. Will you be able to introduce him to your educated friends and mentors without being tempted to hide the fact that he has no degree? If he continues to work at his current job and you decide to pursue your Ph.D., will you be able to love him without resentment and shame? If you always make more money than he does and you find that you are carrying the financial burden throughout the course of your marriage, do you think that he will continue to be enough of a person for you and that you will be able to respect him the way that he deserves to be respected?

2. In addition to a woman accepting her husband, he also needs to accept himself. *Sometimes self-acceptance can be the hardest form of acceptance.* It is hard for a man to feel like a man when he does not feel that he is financially adequate. Many times this, along with his bedroom skills, is what defines who he really is and how he sees himself. Often, when the woman is making more money, the relationship goes through unnecessary stress because the man just can't find his rightful place and purpose in the relationship, even when his mate truly accepts him.

     To many couples' surprise, it takes a strong and confident man to be comfortable, supportive and still valuable in this type of non-traditional marriage. Most couples are successful when the man can find other ways to contribute that bring an equal amount of joy and peace to the marriage. For example, maybe your husband is better domestically than you are or maybe he can take the load of paying the bills off your shoulders and put the family on a realistic budget. Regardless of what it is, it is imperative that he establishes for himself what he can bring that is uniquely his own contribution. This will increase his confidence and lessen the likelihood of your being resentful of him in the future.

3. There is no sense in fooling oneself: Family, friends and relatives are not going to understand why a woman and

her husband have decided on such an imbalanced lifestyle. They are going to think that the woman is settling and that her husband is taking advantage of her. Both the woman and her husband need to come to terms with the fact that people cannot be stopped from talking, wondering and gossiping about their arrangement. *But the more comfortable a woman is in the relationship, the more comfortable outside people will be.* If a woman tries to hide her arrangement, it gives others more to talk about and proves that she is also uncomfortable. If she sees it as a lifestyle that just makes sense for her and her husband, then others are more likely to believe that also.

4. If a woman's husband can't acknowledge, confront and then get help with his own insecurities, it will be almost impossible for the relationship to work. He will be jealous and start holding his wife back. She will resent him for stopping her from being all that she can be. The relationship will start swarming with resentment, envy and sometimes hatred and then this swarm of jealousy will end up destroying the relationship.

If, when you search your soul, you find that you can still accept your husband even if he never pursues a job with more money or never has the desire to get a degree, it is important to tell him that you accept him and that you are satisfied with him if things never change. It is just as important for your husband to tell you that he has no desire to ever hold you back or to stop you from pursuing your dreams and he needs to verbally let you know that he supports you 100 percent.

The belief that all women just want a man who makes more money than they do is simply not true. Many women of the new millennium can afford to buy what they want and numerous progressive women are beginning to appreciate the true value of men who will be faithful and loyal to their families, have their own opinions, show confidence and be humble.

Infidelity

Infidelity is not only highlighted in movie plots, but also it is featured on many of the talk shows and local and national news reports that are supposed to be covering the most important issues of our day. Historically it was much more common for men to be the ones who were involved in outside relationships. However, nowadays more women are unfaithful and have become much more sophisticated at keeping their other relationships secret.

Infidelity is said to be one of the top reasons for breakups. Relationship therapists and sexual addiction counselors advise society to be more understanding and reveal why and how a person can be tangled in a love affair outside of the relationship to which he or she was committed. More scandalous these days is not necessarily having an affair, but instead having liaisons with multiple men or multiple women at the same time while being married; this has become a new major focus. Recent examples are the stories of Tiger Woods, David Letterman, Jesse James and numerous politicians. The rationale for outsiders looking in on these relationships is that one can still be decent, ethical and love one's family while getting tangled in the deception of an affair. Many people believe that it is almost impossible for a man to be faithful and to be able to control himself around seductive and beautiful women. These days it is not so much the affair that is being looked at as being disgusting but what an adulterer does and how he or she corrects the actions once the affair has happened is being judged. To balance out the negative effect of an affair, it is now popular for the one committing infidelity to confess that he or she has a sexual addiction and that is the reason for that person being unfaithful. *It is not uncommon for the cheater to blame the problem on an issue outside of him or herself, instead of just admitting that he or she was attracted to someone else, acted on that attraction and then got caught!*

It is not uncommon for the man to realize that other women don't have the same hang-ups that he feels are present in his relationship with his wife. He becomes attracted to the lightheartedness of other women he sees when he is not at home. He neglects to understand that when his wife is at work or in the grocery store, she acts lighthearted as well. *Just like his wife, the other women whom he encounters are giving their best to the outside world and may be experiencing the same anger and unhappiness at home. Because, as human beings, we tend to connect to what we see and not what we know, it is easy for men to be attracted and then pursue women who seem the opposite of their wives.*

Once he realizes that he has a new attraction he starts giving more attention and energy toward his attraction instead of toward his relationship with his wife. This is usually when an extramarital affair happens. Men start becoming more aware of the personality traits that they no longer find at home and then they start giving extra attention to them; *they become wrapped up in what they see of other women and not what they know of them.*

This problem can also exist when a woman feels that she has outgrown her mate. Men who seemingly look like they have themselves together or make it obvious that they have more to offer than her present husband become very attractive. The admiration can start in how he dresses or the way he carries himself; it does not have to be anything big. She becomes more aware and sensitive to the quality of focus that she finds in other men. Consciously and unconsciously, she gives more attention to them, because they seem intriguing. When she gives attention to other men they return the attention to her—attention that she has not received in a long time on account of the confusion and lack of communication in her own relationship with her husband.

As a society, I believe we try to make infidelity more complex than what it really is. The bottom line is most infidelity happens because of *how the outside person made a partner feel compared to how the partner presently felt with his or her spouse. Other people successfully and naturally bring something to the table that a spouse is not presently getting at home.* The reason behind infidelity holds true for both men and women. "How s/he makes me feel" has been discovered as one of the top reasons why people cheat. Because as human beings we are visual beings we seem to always be shocked when the "other one" is not as attractive as the cheater's current husband or wife. Over and over again we truly seem not to understand that it is more about the "emotional turn on" than the "physical turn on" when it comes to an affair. This doesn't mean that adulterers do not experience physical attraction; this is what causes initial interest and mutual attraction toward each other. Once that is established "how s/he makes me feel" determines if there is going to be an actual affair or not. The bottom line is that it starts out as physical, but then it becomes more emotional in an affair fiasco.

You Can't Keep Someone Who Doesn't Want to be Kept
Daniel and Lil were married over seven years, but had increasing problems because Lil had outgrown Daniel in almost every aspect of their relationship. Before they married, Lil knew that she had the upper hand financially. However, Daniel was constantly telling her how he would "add to her life" in other areas once they got married. For Lil, what bothered her most was the fact that Daniel was very unmotivated

and uninterested in doing better for himself in addition to becoming more of an asset to the family. He lacked vision and goals and felt that it was his right to simply benefit from the hard work and the planning that Lil had done for her life.

After they divorced, Lil was shocked and confused by how much she missed Daniel. She started feeling like although he did not contribute much to the family, that life was more enjoyable with him than without him. Lil realized that she ultimately had the "last word" when it came to their relationship, so after they were divorced for nine months Lil decided to remarry Daniel and try it again.

During the nine months of separation Daniel started really enjoying his freedom and dating multiple women. He had forgotten the fun and the attention that other women gave to him. It was like a vacation having no one nagging him and telling him what he needed to do and how he should act. Because Daniel needed the financial stability that his relationship with Lil provided, he agreed to remarry her. Although Daniel tried, he had a hard time letting go of his admiration for other women. About five weeks after getting remarried, Lil learned of another woman with whom Daniel was still having sexual relations. After a while, Lil realized that Daniel was sleeping and courting multiple women even though they were remarried. Although they decided to go to counseling, Lil did not feel that the counseling helped. It seemed as though whenever they were out together, Daniel looked at women, commented on their beauty and gave other women more attention than he gave her.

Although Lil was embarrassed to do so, she decided to divorce Daniel for the second time. However, she continued to long for Daniel's companionship. Although Daniel was very clear with Lil that he was dating multiple women and sleeping with most of them, Lil started sleeping with him several times a month just so that she could still have a part of him. She knew that her thinking was irrational, but she justified her actions by telling herself that she had no other prospects and that sex with Daniel was safer than having sex with a complete stranger.

It might be a comfort to know that all of us go from being irrational to rational and then back again at different periods of our lives. Usually when we are the most vulnerable and insecure is when we are the most irrational. *Being irrational is part of being normal.*

It is unlikely that Daniel will ever change. He is a person who has caused frustration, confusion and heartbreak from the beginning. It was a grave mistake for Lil to think that that she was going to get more from Daniel once they were married. Regardless of what a man promises, if the application of fulfilling those promises does not happen before the marriage it is very unlikely that it will happen after the marriage. *The promise to do better after the marriage should have been Lil's first warning sign.* He initially would not carry his weight in the relationship and was unmotivated to try to do better; *this should have been Lil's second warning sign.* It was clear at this point that Daniel was not 100 percent committed to the marriage and the work needed to create a healthy relationship. Daniel's lack of effort supports that he did not have much interest in Lil and her personal happiness even before the infidelity took place.

Women can't keep someone who does not want to be kept. Daniel has a love for the lifestyle of a single man. In this exam- ple, there are no consequences for Daniel's lack of motivation and unfaithfulness. Lil has successfully trained him how to treat her. Many times it seems that having an affair is more disloyal than not pulling one's weight in the relationship but the source of the mindset is from the same place. This mindset suggests that a person is more concerned about the needs of himself than his wife and that he really doesn't care what outcome his actions will bring.

Daniel only decided to remarry Lil because of her financial advantage. *If that is the reason why he remarried her then that is also the reason why he has stayed with her: simply because she has what he needs.* Daniel is the one with the upper edge and advantage in this situation. He can have the perks of a relationship with Lil as well as other women. Although Lil may verbally disagree and argue, because she decides to sleep with him knowing that there are other women, it gives Daniel permission to continue in the affairs. *When a person has repeated affairs and his mate is aware of them without cheating herself, this relationship is defined as a one-sided open relationship.* It teaches Daniel that despite the hurt that Lil may experience through his actions, it obviously does not hurt that bad because she continues to be with him. Daniel continuing with his affairs should have been Lil's third warning sign.

Ultimately it is Lil's responsibility to think for and respect herself. *It is not anyone else's responsibility to keep reminding Lil that she can do better.*

Lil says she remains with Daniel despite his relationships with other women because of the sex. I challenge this perspective. I believe that Lil is with Daniel because she feels addicted to being with him and lonely. It is not about the sex; it is the ideal of Lil feeling like she belongs to someone and that she is in a relationship despite how dysfunctional it is. It is more about Lil's personal self-esteem than her need for sex.

There are some people who are just not interested or mature enough to settle down and be happy with one person. Regardless of Daniel's reason for his unfaithfulness and lack of motivation, at this point it really does not matter; he is neither "in love enough" or "committed enough" to be loyal in this relationship with Lil.

He is Perfect to Someone Else

How many women would change their negative tones toward their husbands if they realized that someone else in the world would be satisfied with their husbands and who they are? Maybe this would not matter for some, but it would make a profound difference for many others. *Too many times women assume that because they don't want their husbands no one else will.* We are not talking about a man who is an abuser or even a person who is morally corrupt; we are talking about a man who has lost his way and no longer knows how to make his wife happy and to make his own self complete. While a woman is in the situation of feeling that she has outgrown her husband, it can easily seem like things could never get any worse because her entire focus becomes what he is not and what he does not bring.

However, when he is involved in an affair he shows his best self to the other woman, because he does not have the responsibilities and obligations with the other woman that he does to his wife. At this level, it is all about enjoying each other's company like it was at the beginning of his relationship with his wife. The other woman is not focused on what he doesn't bring to the table; she is consumed with what he does bring. In many cases, these days, the other woman knows that he is married and not looking to leave his family, so she is not necessarily looking at him to be marriage material; she simply wants him to be companionship material. More and more women are becoming so desperate to have men in their lives they are happy to settle for having someone around some of the time.

The problem with this is that he starts feeling more confident and secure around his lover and he feels that she is actually someone whom he "needs" in his life. He stops seeing himself as the one who needs to change; now he really starts to believe that the problem is with his wife and that she is just sour and bitter, especially since his lover can so easily see the value in him. *His lover's validation of him just supports that he is not actually the problem but that his situation with his wife is the problem.* All he really needed was to be around someone different. *His lover does not complain, nag or get upset; their relationship is simply full of fun, sex and togetherness—exactly how it used to be with his wife.*

Every woman is not looking for the same thing. What is good for one may not be satisfying to another. Many stressed out women do need for their husbands to help with the tasks and responsibilities of the household and to contribute fairly to the needs of the family, but some women simply are seeking companions. Many women would prefer to have both but the idea of that starts becoming more of a fantasy. A woman's experiences and what she has gone through in her life will often determine what she needs and wants in her present situation. Sometimes it can be refreshing to have someone who can be there when she comes home from work or someone with whom she can go out and have dinner. Infidelity can be hurtful to relationships, so remember that often what can be your curse can easily be viewed as someone else's blessing!

The reality is that when infidelity comes into the picture a woman now has a bigger, more devastating problem than simply outgrowing her husband. If she decides to stay in the relationship, the major issues become being able to trust again, overcoming resentment and trying to find out if the relationship is strong enough to overcome the damage of his affair.

4

Deception

Life Will Never Give More than Asked For
Rich and Kay had been high school sweethearts, had been married for almost seven years and have a son together. Rich had started a new job and began expressing his problems from home to another woman. Within months, Rich left Kay and Kay was served divorce papers out of nowhere. Kay discovered that her relationship was a deceptive one; Rich was cheating on her and, soon after, Rich married the other woman.

Although Kay was upset with Rich they started talking every night on the phone and developed the friendship they had forgotten about during their marriage. Before long, Rich started sharing with Kay his present problems with his new wife. According to him, his new marriage was horrible. Rich told Kay that he did not believe his relationship with his second wife would last due to many complex issues.

Even though he was remarried with two children, Rich regretted everything he had done to Kay. He apologized to

Kay for breaking her heart and not being a man of his word when he vowed loyalty, trust and love. He explained to Kay that he had been naïve, young and immature and that he never should have left her. He also admitted that he felt threatened by Kay, who he felt seemed to have her life so together and planned. Rich had not felt like he had much purpose and meaning in their marriage because Kay made it obvious that she could handle everything without him. Rich never told Kay how he felt while they were married because he thought Kay already knew. He asked Kay if she would give him another chance if he divorced his wife.

Deep down Kay still desired to be with her husband and was not sure what to do. She feared that she would not be able to trust him and that his feelings of "not being enough" would simply grow. But she was very scared to let go of the "ideal" of marriage and of never having a man in her life again.

Regardless of how many times a person marries, infidelity is a hurtful, horrible and an unfair monster that is destructive in many ways. When a woman's first and only true love betrays her, it can be devastating and it can easily make her question her past and her future.

As in most relationships, reflecting on the story of Kay and Rich does not present definite answers or an easy way out. Here are some key aspects Kay and Rich need to consider:

♦ The fact that Rich served Kay divorce papers without any verbal discussion is a sneaky and cowardly way to approach any conflict. It would have been different if Rich had talked with Kay about his concerns or if he had encouraged counseling to try and fix the relationship before leaving. He made no effort to fix what he had; instead he was simply trying to please his new lover. In most cases, it is the new mistress pushing for marriage and commitment, not the adulterous husband.

♦ Rich blames part of the reason why he left Kay on the fact that he was young. Only a few years have passed in his new marriage, so Kay should question how much Rich has truly grown. If he is willing to do to his new wife exactly what he did to Kay, he can't have changed too much and should not be fully trusted.

♦ Kay needs to realize that Rich now comes with a much more complex package than when he left her. Kay needs to accept that Rich now has the emotional, physical and financial responsibility of two other children. If Kay remarries Rich and Rich should lose his job, Kay may be financially liable for child support for these two children. In addition, Rich will have an ongoing relationship with his ex-wife and their children for many years to come. Kay needs to reflect on whether she can adjust to the fact that Rich has other children who have just as much right to be with their father as her own son does.

♦ It seems a shame for Rich to be able to walk back into Kay's life so easily. I believe there should be some type of consequence for what he has done to their relationship. *People learn through consequences.* Kay's willingness to be Rich's friend and consider taking him back when he betrayed her and is still married to someone else reflects on Kay's self-esteem. It also shows that neither Kay nor Rich have learned much from their past mistakes.

An important thing Kay needs to realize is that more than likely what Rich is telling Kay about his horrible marriage with his new wife is also most likely what he told his present wife about his marriage with Kay. To fully reflect on Rich's offer, Kay and other women in her situation should ask themselves these questions:

- What type of father has he been to our children in the years since the divorce? Has he been involved or not around? This answer will reveal a lot about a man's personal character.
- Would I truly be able to forgive, forget and move on or would I live a life of suspicion and paranoia if I remarried him?
- Would I be able to accept his new children and treat them fairly as being part of our family without having ill feelings towards them?
- Do I feel that my consideration of allowing him back in my life is really a sign of insecurity and the fear of being left alone?
- Is he the type of man who always has to be with a woman? Or would he be willing to get out of his present relationship, live alone, work on his own personal issues and then evaluate the relationship after some time alone?
- If I am currently having sex with my ex-husband, does he love and respect me enough to be willing to stop having sex until he can commit himself totally to me or is intimacy a requirement to having a relationship with him now?

Life will give you no more than what you ask for. If you are willing to accept a part-time lover, that is all you will ever get.

Minimizing Success
The husband holds unspoken power when he is able to support the family financially. If the man is consistently the breadwinner financially regardless of how many areas his wife thinks that she has outgrown him, the wife tends to stay in the relationship.

Although a woman may outgrow her mate in one or two aspects of the relationship, in many cases her husband still provides a substantial income that she can count on week after week. Or he may provide a higher economic status than what she would enjoy if she was alone, which can overshadow any complaints that she may also have. In some situations, a man's higher economic status allows the couple to choose whether a woman is going to work outside the home or stay home with her children.

Because financial and social power have the most influence in our society, the need for more well-rounded mates has only recently come to the surface and become more prevalent. This pressure is mostly put on by oneself, society and the media.

In most cases successful women are looking for long-term commitments, possibly marriage, not simply bed partners. If they are willing to start by being "less than" honest about their success in order to meet mates, they will more than likely continue to downplay and be "less than" honest in their entire relationships.

Many women want men who are not threatened by their success but who can celebrate what the two of them have accomplished both separately and together. Many women would agree that really what they are looking for is a man who is secure enough to accept his woman in all of her bliss and success; who is confident enough in himself to do whatever he does with excellence; who truly understands that the more confident he is the more confident the relationship will be as a whole; who knows that if she is more successful, it is not necessarily due to ability but instead it may be due to the choices she has decided to make for herself.

Although it is a growing trend for women to feel the need to downplay their true accomplishments, the results of such a game can prove to be devastating. First, it is not fair to either the man or the woman if she decides to diminish her accomplishments. It is not fair for her to assume that he can't handle her success and it is even more unfair to assume that he does not have equal or even more success than her. To decide before even meeting a man that there is a need for a woman to downplay what she has accomplished shows that she is already expecting him to be her lesser.

The reality of this rub is that when you pose yourself as "less than" and then later in a relationship show that you are really "more than," it starts the relationship on untruth and it causes resentment and insecurity in the male that may not have originally been there. Secondly, it is not fair to the accomplished female in the beginning. To have to pose as someone you are not just to make a man more comfortable will make you uncomfortable. That game can only be played for so long. After some time the discomfort the woman feels will turn to resentment in later years. She will start resenting the fact that she has felt that she has had to sacrifice her accomplishment for him.

Hard to Find a Job
Rochelle is a black, successful, hardworking female who has been an assistant school principal for seven years. She has been married to Ken for thirteen years and he is also hardworking. He is contract construction worker who is presently out of work and struggling with finding new jobs to keep himself employed. They have created a beautiful life together: They have two children, Rochelle makes a good wage and Ken makes double Rochelle's salary when he is working.

Although Ken is smart, dependable and a great husband and father, Rochelle is frustrated with Ken's inability to keep consistent work. His employers love him when he is hired but because he works on a contract basis, he rarely has consistent work and the contracts usually do not last any longer than twelve months at one time. Ken is finding that getting hired is becoming more and more difficult. He often wonders if the reason why contractors are reluctant to hire him is because he's a black man. He has noticed that several of his white colleagues get work much quicker.

Rochelle has become increasingly frustrated because Ken is constantly out of work and she finds that she has the entire financial responsibility. She finds it hard to believe that Ken is unable to find work because he is black, because Ken has rave reviews from his past contract work. He is out looking for work every day but can only find occasional jobs. Although Rochelle does not 100 percent believe that Ken is discriminated against, lately she has been comparing herself to her white coworkers who seem to have an easier path than she does. It seems like she has had to work harder and much longer hours just to prove that she is a team player. Although everyone is nice, when she expresses anger or frustration just like anyone else at her workplace, her coworkers tend to be fearful that she is going to take it too far. She has never come close to exploding her anger before, but there is an underlying fear in her department that she has hidden "black anger."

Ken actually has a four-year college degree while many of his contemporaries don't have degrees at all yet still seem to be able to find and keep work. Rochelle wonders if the media has plagued her husband, like it has most black men, and has caused others to view him as just another black male who is up to no good. This problem develops tension and confusion in their relationship. Rochelle feels embarrassed and resentful toward her husband and wonders if he is trying to take advantage of her and just not work. She is confused whether the problem is his fault or society's fault. She finds that their sex life and line of communication have started suffering drastically.

Without knowing it, Ken has started making the same mistake that many men do when they are out of work. Instead of looking for additional ways that he can make his wife's life easier as she goes to work every day—keeping the house clean, doing the grocery shopping, cooking dinner, helping the children with their homework—he slips into a depression, shuts down, stops communicating and feels that his wife has prejudged him just like everyone else. After three years of dealing with the same struggle, Ken and Rochelle both agree that they don't have any more energy or interest to commit to the relationship and decide to end their marriage.

Ken and Rochelle are fighting a societal belief and stereotypes. Although this should not have any power in Rochelle and Ken's marriage, because he is not able to find work, his entire character is questioned due to stereotypes. The problem with stereotypes is that they do not allow for normal unfortunate circumstances to happen to those people the stereotypes target and it makes it very unfair when regular things happen to "regular" people. Despite what society and the media has said about the downfall and the increasing rise of "no good black men," Rochelle needs to look beyond her husband's circumstance and see his situation outside of what society has already said about him. Ken also is internally fighting with what he should already know about himself. The saying, "All men are dogs" may not have meant much to Ken before his work issues but after years and years of struggling to be gainfully employed, it is only realistic to start looking at himself and wondering if there is a little "dog" in himself. With both Rochelle and Ken there is that extra pressure that they will have to overcome. The stereotypes influence what the couple already knows and filters in to become what they believe.

As we discussed previously, most men base their self-worth on what they do and how much money they make. And after years of Ken struggling to make money and establish meaning in his life, it has taken a personal toll on his family life, work life and overall self-esteem.

It is somewhat understandable that Ken would be extra hard on himself and start questioning his life and personal path, but for Rochelle to also wonder about the character of Ken is unfortunate and is a result of the stereotypes. It seems clear that Ken is a good, hardworking, faithful father and husband who is well liked and respected by his employers. Ken and Rochelle have been married for thirteen years and his loyalty and personality have proven to be consistent.

Why would the problem of Ken finding a job make his wife question his personal character and the integrity that he has already proven? When Rochelle knows that he is spending every day looking for a job, why would she still blame him for not finding work? Ken is her husband of thirteen years, not a new boyfriend about whom she does not know anything. He has proven that he is not lazy and not trying to get out of working. She should not be embarrassed, but rather stand strong on the fact that Ken has proven himself for the past thirteen years.

However, it was Ken who has probably made the biggest mistake that resulted in the deterioration of his marriage. Yes, there is frustration and tension that naturally comes when one spouse is out of work and these tend to escalate when it is the husband. But if Ken had looked around at what he could have given back to his family during this time of hardship, he could have restored his wife's positive image of him. He was not working, but Ken could have cooked dinner every night, made sure that the house was clean, made sure the bills were paid on time and helped the kids with their homework, which would have taken a lot of responsibility from Rochelle. When a wife works hard during the day and then comes home only to work harder at home in the evenings, she has the tendency to feel used and taken for granted. If Rochelle had known that while she was at work Ken loved and respected her enough to make her life easier when she got home, her overall admiration and respect may have increased for him. She would have seen his willingness to help around the house as a sign of true love for her. Working every day and bringing in money is expected and not seen as anything special. But being the man of the house and willing to do the household duties is completely unexpected and tends to get more attention, which is some-thing that Ken needed to save his marriage.

The Emotional Side of Outgrowth

Let's now look at how this outgrowth might have begun in the early stages of life. There has been much discussion and research supporting that boys, through the things they do, show themselves to be less mature than girls. Girls outgrow what is viewed as childish play and games sooner than boys of the same age. Girls also become interested in romantic relationships at a younger age than boys. Such interests reflect girls' abilities to focus and adopt a serious mindset. Could it be that "the maturity argument hinges implicitly on matters pertaining to relationships"? It is possible that a child's maturity happens when he or she first expresses interest in relationships?[1]

If this is true, it brings up a very interesting topic. Thinking back, when a guy is interested in dating numerous girls this does not result in a rise in maturity. On the other hand, when a guy falls deeply in love with one specific girl, he does seem to become more focused and more centered about what he is doing and where he is going. It is not uncommon to see his

confidence increase and him speaking up in defense of his relationship with his first love. Many times he will become less
available to his friends and colleagues. The seriousness of the
relationship will cause him to look at his spending habits and
what he is doing overall in his life. It is common that a serious
and loving relationship with a woman can often rush a man
into being a more mature person. It can also help him not
spend his free time in the streets with his friends, because he is
busy being with his love. It is not uncommon for parents to
feel more comfortable with their son's whereabouts when he
becomes serious with a girlfriend. They often start feeling
relieved especially if their son had the tendency to hang around
with the wrong crowd or not make good choices. Having a
girlfriend can give him a place to be and many times keep him
off the streets and out of trouble.

When does society start judging whether a person is mature
or not? Most often it is when one reaches puberty. Although
it is rare to question maturity in pubesence, it is becoming
more common to many parents and educators that their
daughters are born serious, business and no-nonsense and their
boys come into the world sweet, innocent and loving.

Even the survival rate of premature babies suggests a
stronger fight in girls versus boys and this much earlier than
puberty: "Extremely premature baby girls were 1.7 times more
likely to survive than baby boys."[2] This finding, which continues to cause confusion and raise questions, suggests a strength
that is actually there before the baby is even born.

This whole notion of maturity brings up intriguing questions, but I am still a believer that the way our children are
raised has a lasting impact on how fast they mature. If a son is
taught that he does not have to play soccer because he is afraid
of getting hurt then he might have the tendency not to push
himself when it comes to challenges and opposition in his life.

When a daughter is taught early to wash clothes, do the dishes and shop for groceries, she learns how to take care of her basic needs without needing to depend on others.

How much of the maturity argument has power simply because we have been conditioned to believe that it is true? Could the reason why mothers tend to love their boys instead of teach them be because they believe that boys are less mature and need to be nurtured? Could the reason why women tend to teach their girls be because mothers believe that girls can take it and that they are emotionally tough? How much of this maturity argument is simply a *self-fulfilling prophecy. A man is less mature because he believes that he would be and a woman is more mature because she was taught that she is supposed to be.*

It would be unfair to label one thing as the sole reason why boys tend to need more time developing than girls, but I think most of us would agree that just two or three combinations of beliefs and habits can be enough to alter one's maturity level.

We can see this emotional imbalance in our children when they are very young. Too often emotionally insecure kids grow up to be emotionally insecure adults whereas secure kids result in secure adults.

Fraud and Lying

Fraud: "A false representation of a matter of fact, whether by words or by conduct, by false or misleading allegations, or by concealment of that which should have been disclosed, which deceives and is intended to deceive another so that he shall act upon it."[3]

While it may be necessary for some people to lie, even on a daily basis, chronic lying in a romantic relationship often suggests deceit, addiction and/or infidelity.

Here are some possible signs of lying collected by Sheri and Bob Stritof, journalists on marriage:[4]

- Touching chin, or rubbing their brows.
- A line of perspiration on the brow if it isn't a warm day.
- Saying "no" several times.
- Continual denying of accusations.
- Being extremely defensive.
- Providing more information and specifics than is necessary or was asked for.
- Inconsistencies in what is being shared.
- Body language and facial expressions don't match what is being said such as saying "no", but nodding head up and down.
- May place a barrier such as a desk or chair in front of self.
- Unwillingness to touch spouse during conversation.
- Differing behaviors. Not acting in a usual fashion.
- Unusual voice fluctuations, word choice, sentence structure.
- Stalling the conversation by repetitive use of pauses and comments like "um" or "you know".
- Lack of use of contractions. Prefers emphasizing "not" when talking.
- Avoidance of eye contact, eyes glancing to the right, staring past you, or turning away from you while they are talking.

It is difficult to advise a woman what to do when she believes her partner is lying. Each woman needs to consider her individual situation and relationship to determine the best course of action. Some women may prefer to wait and gather more information and other women may want to confront partners immediately about their lying. Women should ask their partners for clarification about things and trust their own intuitions.

When people appear too good to be true, they usually are. No one is perfect. No one's life is without flaw. Many times a woman will fall into an unrealistic situation and believe that she has found the perfect man, that finally she has met her Prince Charming. But realistically, Prince Charming is a myth and the entire concept of a perfect man is simply untrue. If the person a woman thinks is Prince Charming is perfect in one area then she can be assured that he is not in another. I think we all can agree that there are hidden secrets in all the people whom we meet. It does not necessarily mean that something is horribly wrong with them. The reason could simply be the one or two things that they personally struggle with on an everyday basis. It could be overeating or feeling the need to control. It's not that he isn't a good person with a good heart and really good intentions, but for a woman to assume that she has met a person who has no flaws and no faults will only be proved untrue and cause hardship in the future. To actually believe that he is incredibly handsome, emotionally and financially strong, spiritually fit, intellectually competitive and highly confident without any personal issues is a fairy tale. Many women and men feel fascinated to be with someone extremely good looking and they forget about all the qualities that they bring to the relationship. Regardless of how big or small, no one is perfect and there are some flaws in every person, just as people will discover some in you.

Remember, we all have the tendency to make ourselves look as glowing and marketable as we can when we meet someone we are trying to impress; this is human nature. We all can probably puff up and slightly exaggerate our attributes and the things that we offer without actually telling boldface lies about ourselves. But when we intentionally lie or talk about our pasts as if our illusions and rationalizations are realities, this is a dangerous game to play.

Should Women Make the First Move?
Many women find it difficult to find a good and available man. More and more women are not sitting around waiting for men to approach and pursue them; rather, they are boldly taking

the lead. Of course, traditionally it has always been the man who approaches the woman so many women feel a bit embarrassed and uncomfortable being the initiator.

Although this new approach to dating is becoming more acceptable, there is a definite long-term disadvantage that women are facing with this new way of thinking. In relationships, it is too often true that *once the initiator always the initiator.* Initially, however, many women find that being the first one to pursue a man may be the only way to meet the men of their dreams. Men are getting use to the idea that women now approach men and due to this fact, they are much slower to approach women because they feel they don't have to. Many men also tend to fear being rejected and if they don't approach women first they don't have to worry about being turned down. Men oftentimes are intimidated by confident and beautiful women and may desire to approach them but are too fearful of rejection. *The more women take the initiative to pursue men, the less other men will feel the need to approach women.* In most cases younger women are complaining that there is a new wave of arrogance among young men, because they feel that they are the sought after commodity and have the advantage. Some believe that when a woman is the first one to approach a man, it suggests that he has the upper hand and control of where the relationship will end up. *He has the power to say yes or no to the relationship.* There is then a belief that she is the vulnerable and most interested one. In the past, the man who approached the woman was carrying out the man's role. He did not seem desperate; he just appeared interested. The woman being approached knew that in her era this was the proper protocol. This established her as being the "yes" person in the relationship that we discussed in chapter 2.

Whether it is a new level of personal power in women, role reversal between men and women or a fear from women that approaching men is their last hope, flirtation in women has reached a new level of intensity. It has gone from making eye contact to direct verbal approach. In some cases, women who begin a relationship by approaching men are also asking for the first date, calling men the most and usually remain the most vulnerable emotionally throughout the relationship. Women who act like this establish themselves as the aggressors. When this initial introduction develops into love and then turns into marriage, I believe this approach becomes a long-term disadvantage. Most women view being the initiator as a way to possibly meet Mr. Right and don't realize that being the aggressor initially means that they will need to be the initiator forever.

As the relationship deepens, in many cases women become tired of being expected to be the first one to do everything. They become frustrated when they have to schedule all the dates nights or initiate hand holding or cuddling. This becomes an area of disharmony and imbalance in the relationship. She starts complaining that he is not carrying his load or that she does not feel loved or appreciated. When this situation becomes intolerable the female starts expecting her husband to do a role reversal overnight and become the pursuer. She neglects to realize that *she has taught her husband how to treat her, love her and be in a relationship with her by what she has traditionally expected from him.* The first time they met and she approached him she began teaching him that she did not mind taking the role of the pursuer. As the relationship deepened, the woman often noticed that she was the pursuer, the aggressor and the one who was the most vulnerable emotionally. When you also add the complications of the imbalance that women often complain about with the feeling of being the one who has to initiate everything, it is understandable that the wife feels cheated and dissatisfied with her marriage.

5

Relationship Stages

The Ten Phases of Relationships

My husband of twenty-four years once explained to my son the dynamics of keeping a strong relationship. He explained that it is impossible for a relationship to begin unless one *meets* the person first. It is important to recognize that meeting has to be a personal encounter. It is more than just saying hello to a passing person in the shopping mall and being smitten. The type of meeting needed is formal, not informal. To guard oneself from hurt in the future, it is imperative to understand that everyone somebody meets is not available *and everyone one meets one is not supposed to like.* Many women argue that meeting an eligible man can be most difficult, especially if he is a "good catch." Female clients have reported to me that in many cases the more attractive the person is, the harder he is to actually meet and the less likely he is to make eye contact. Unfortunately in our society, we actually expect "beautiful people" to be standoffish or aloof. We have the tendency to believe that the less attractive, low confidence or extensively overweight person tends to be goofy, talkative or extra jolly. In my research in meeting with clients, I have found that the ease or difficulty of meeting someone worthwhile has very little to do with specific gender; it has more to do with a combination of confidence level, communication skills and level of humility.

Their confidence makes them attractive, their communication reflects their ease with talking to others and their humility allows them to be approachable. So the belief that the most attractive people are the ones who are the most difficult to meet on a personal basis is not necessarily true. Just as it is not true that the more average the person the easier he or she is to meet.

The second stage is to *like* the person. It is imperative to understand that in this phase the word *like* is meant very superficially. After meeting a person, ask yourself a few questions:

♦ Do I feel at ease with the person?
♦ Do I find this person attractive?
♦ Am I initially comfortable with the person's body language and how I feel when I am around him?

At this phase, a person has very little on which to base any kind of tangible opinion. The main indicators are the physical attributes, such as specific body language or possibly how the person interacts with other people. Both the man and the woman need to answer each of the questions positively before the next stage should be considered.

When both parties successfully give signals that they like each other, historically, the man will pursue the female for a *date*. It is most imperative to understand in this stage the role of each person. Although things are rapidly changing, traditionally men have been the pursuers and women have been the "yes" people. The man usually asks the questions and the woman is responsible for responding. She determines what will or will not occur. In the past she had to respond "yes" to giving him her telephone number and she had to say "yes" to going on a date. Ultimately she is the one who says "yes" to marriage. Today, out of sheer desperateness, a fear of being alone or a newfound boldness, many women pursue men and ask them for their telephone numbers or out on dates. Unfortunately, many couples find that once the woman relinquishes her "yes" power by making herself the pursuer and allowing the man to have the privilege of saying no, she continues to be the one pursuing all the way through their relationship. When this happens a woman starts feeling resentful and unappreciated. Deep down she feels that the roles have been switched and that she is not receiving but instead giving.

After a while, the woman who is the pursuer may start wondering why her personal emotions seem to always be on the line. From dating, then the engagement all the way to the marriage, her emotions are more displayed and vulnerable than her husband's. She finds a pattern where she is usually the one who initiates the words *I love you.* She starts desiring for him to open the car door for her or to initiate romantic getaways, but she finds year after year that special moments happen because of her planning. *She neglects to understand that when the woman pursues, it teaches the man that he does not have to.* It is not fair to teach your mate that you will be the pursuer at the beginning and then expect him to know when to take over and start pursuing later in the relationship.

During dating, it is the couple's responsibility to either confirm or dismiss the initial feelings they had in the beginning phases. I call this the *confirmation* phase. The relationships that don't turn into meaningful experiences usually end at this stage. It is common for both parties to desire physical intimacy during this time. Many women will say "yes" to sex in hopes that their relationships will develop deeper or sometimes they are afraid that the men will lose interest in the relationships unless they have sex with them. *Sometimes, having sex at this stage ends the relationship and stops the additional developmental stages from happening.* After sex, many times some men lose interest in women, because they feel that they have discovered everything worth discovering about the women. Unlike many males, after sex, many females start becoming emotionally attached and start feeling like they have deeper relationships than they actually do. This causes women to react with more control, emotions and passion than before. Many times, they wrongly assume that men are more attached to them than the men actually are. After sex, women may believe that they are exclusive couples, even without verbal commitment, when they are simply dating. It is not uncommon for men to start pulling away as women become more controlling.

The more he resists her, the harder she pursues him. She wants to be around him more. She questions his whereabouts and relationship involvement with other people. *She does not realize that the more questions she asks the more emotionally unavailable he becomes.* When the relationship has dwindled down to nothing, she starts feeling resentful, taken for granted and angry because she has now sexually given a part of herself that she can never get back.

If they separate, the woman has the tendency to blame the man for leaving soon after sexual relations and she neglects to understand the power she had before in keeping herself as the "yes" person instead of turning into the "giver." If the couple doesn't separate and the relationship continues to the next phase, it has a very good chance of becoming meaningful for a very long time.

This next phase occurs when the couple *becomes friends.* This can bind and keep the relationship functional when all else fails. In most romantic relationships, couples never achieve this phase. *Although it is the most important part of the relationship it has also become the most ignored phase.* The reason why most couples never achieve this phase is because, more often than not, both the man and the woman are rushing to get what each *really* wants. For the man, many times he is in a rush to experience the woman sexually. The woman, on the other hand, is busy rushing to figure out if the man could possibly be "the one." Because both people have their own individual goals in mind, developing a friendship seems so unimportant and unexciting at the time. But it is important that this is the one area that couples don't rush into. It demands time. It is a time to sit and listen to the other person and ask questions that help the couple understand each other.

Most couples don't realize that once this phase is truly accomplished there is a bond that will last forever; this is when both people unconsciously separate their romantic interest and replace it with an interest that involves genuine care and concern for their mates. Time is spent asking and answering questions about each other's past and present lives as well as future dreams. Both parties start entrusting each other with truths about their lives that they hold sacred—truths they have learned to only share with special people in their lives. Through time and conversation this is the phase when trust and respect develop, a love for each other's well-being is achieved and the relationship becomes selfless. It becomes more about the other person than about self.

Although most relationships jump into *commitment* without becoming friends first, there is much more contentment and harmony exchanged between the couple when friendship has been established. *Husbands are not quick to have affairs when they first have established friendship with their wives.* This is the phase when both parties mutually agree that they will be exclusive to each other. In contrast to the like and becoming friends phases, this level requires an actual verbal agreement so that there is no misunderstanding between the partners. It has proven to be disastrous when one party thinks the couple is exclusive and the other mate feels that he or she is free to date other people. It is imperative that this stage should not be forced by either party. When one of the parties feels that he or she has no choice in the matter, it is very likely that although the person says he or she will be loyal and exclusive, in most cases he or she will not.

The two parties should not agree to commitment until both of them are satisfied with the other emotionally, physically, intellectually, socially and spiritually. In the commitment stage, all these areas will be challenged. There should be an understanding that the relationship shared by this couple cannot be easily replaced by another. *That is why during this process each party must be willing to pass up other potential mates, because they understand that what they have in each other is indeed special and irreplaceable.*

Discovery is the next phase that is necessary before marriage is considered. Most couples don't realize that it can be disastrous to ignore discovery.

This phase is imperative because couples start discovering several things about each other. Partners learn how they relate to other people not individually but as a couple. They discover how friends interact with the two of them. Couples discover how partners interact with each other's friends, which will affect each partner's personal relationship with his or her friends. Family is another strong consideration in this phase. Friends and family start recognizing the pair as a couple. In the like phase it is common for friends and family not to express much of an opinion about a mate, because they have no idea how serious the relationship will get. In the discovery phase, mothers, fathers and other family members give a strong sense of how they connect to partners' new mates. The family starts to realize in this phase that the partners are serious about each other. When family and friends finally understand that a bond and a possible love have developed, they often become more verbal about their opinions. It is common to see strong feelings from others, either positive or negative, start to form. There is usually stress for the couple in this phase, because the opinion of close friends and family can easily determine the longevity of the relationship. Their opinions will either add to the harmony of the relationship and confirm the positive thoughts the couple is already feeling or add confusion and doubt and make the couple question areas that they thought were fine. The closer the outside people are to each partner, the more likely they are to influence each partner's thoughts about this new relationship.

During the period of discovery, important questions need to be considered. If you don't already know the answer to these questions it is definitely time to find out:

♦ What type of problems does each partner have on his or her credit report that can influence future purchases together?

♦ Does each partner have a desire to have children and if so, how soon after marriage?

♦ What is each partner's life plan for the next five years?

♦ What is each partner's ultimate dream for the future?

♦ What belief system does each person hold politically, spiritually and ethically?

This is the time to explore the other person's financial maturity, his or her level of purchasing control and what emotional power drives the person to purchase things. Does the person impulsively buy or does he or she use sound judgment and long-term planning?

This may sound picky and overly intrusive, but money problems are a major contributor to divorce. *The other person's ability to handle money will either add to the couple's happiness or subtract from it if the partners marry.* For example, if a woman's credit rating is 800, this enables her to buy almost anything. But if her mate's score is a 500, this can stop the couple from buying most things and may cause long-term resentment and problems in the relationship. To know that marrying a person will lessen your chances of getting some of the material pleasures you want in life should be a major consideration.

It is also the opportune period to look at how the other person resolves conflict, not only internally but also with other people. Is the person's reasoning fair and logical? Does the mate show a pattern of blaming someone else or does the person have a sensible perspective that also includes analyzing his or her own actions and motives? Pay special attention to how comfortable the other person is with saying "I'm sorry" and how willing the partner is to forgive others. It is so important that a mate is willing to humble himself enough to say that he has been wrong. Does the mate have the tendency to hold a grudge or can he or she really forgive and let go? It is disastrous to have a partner who will not allow the other partner to live down a mistake made years ago. Bringing up a partner's mistakes in every future argument is unfair.

It can be just as disappointing to have a mate who is quick to say "I'm sorry" without true introspection and to give apologies with meaningless words. True honesty and authenticity is key in this stage; without it a long-term relationship is doomed for destruction.

As a woman questions and seeks the answers to her mate's ability to spend money with maturity, resolve conflict fairly and let go of hurt and resentment, it is just as important to analyze her own self in these areas. To expect a mate to add to a partner's life in these areas is simply unfair if the partner is not also mature enough to add to his own. Many people are skilled at identifying what other people are lacking and need to improve on without truly analyzing their own faults and weaknesses.

One of the most valuable things a couple can do is to experience each other during every phase of emotion. It is common for couples to restrain from contributing to serious arguments or strong disagreements during this time of discovery. To many couples' surprise, it is actually the ideal time for disagreements and arguments to occur. It is the appropriate time to see how the other person truly feels. A healthy, fulfilling relationship requires both a balance of restraint and brutal honesty. It is a great time to determine what a mate is like when he or she is fearful, angry, depressed and disappointed and how a mate reacts when the other partner is hurt or has strong feelings of rejection. In most cases, people react with a normal amount of emotions, which causes no reason for alarm; however, there are those extreme cases when a person just can't tolerate a certain emotion. Anger, by far, is the most uncontrollable and obvious emotion.

When a person has a problem controlling anger, it is not uncommon that he verbally or physically abuses a partner or someone else. Extreme agitation is a clear sign that there can be a future problem in this area. *It is always best to assume that whatever negative problem that is noticeable before marriage will escalate after marriage.* Many times, people make the mistake of believing that they can fix their mates' problems, love their mates out of depression or guide their mates out of anger, but this is not true. *Who a partner is before the marriage will be who he is after the marriage.*

Depression is another major emotion that can sabotage relationships. It is important that mates have resilience, faith and endurance during personal hardships. It is key that they have strength within themselves on which they can rely during challenging times and that they are not looking to partners or other family members for guidance and answers. Mates must gain what they need from within themselves.

It is unfair in a relationship if one partner completely shuts down when depressed and becomes unable to work, eat or even get out of bed. More and more we are hearing about a depression-based mental illness known as bipolar disorder. In such cases, the individual is not able to function in everyday life. When this disorder afflicts one partner, it can be devastating to the healthy mate. It is difficult to plan dates and daily functions because the healthy mate is not sure if the other mate is going to be depressed that day. Although the other emotions we've discussed are important, anger and depression are the two emotions more likely to affect the longevity of a relationship.

During the discovery phase, it is the best time to also find out how a partner defines the word *commitment* and what it means to him. A woman should find out how well she will be able to trust the other person, not only with herself but also with her secrets. This is a good time to see how her mate reacts when he is around other attractive people. Does he have the tendency to stare at others and ignore her? Is he attentive to his partner exclusively, to the point that she doesn't have to compete with beautiful people because he gives the most attention to her? Does he make her feel like she is the most important person in the room? Do the love and affection continue despite whom the couple is around? Or does it seem that he is trying to hide her and her relationship around certain people or situations?

One sure way to discover how committed a mate is to his partner is to observe how he introduces her to his friends. *How he introduces his partner to others is key as to how he wants other people to view their relationship.* If he introduces his partner as a friend, that is exactly the level of commitment with which he is comfortable. *I have found that there is more truth about how partners feel about each other in a mere introduction than a thousand words.* I believe the ultimate truth teller is how he refers to his partner with others when his partner is not around. This reveals how he really feels about the relationship.

The next phase is the *proposal* and during this time a major mistake may be made. Many believe that they should just relax and that there is nothing to do in this period but plan their blissful future together. Although planning for the actual wedding is a large part of this stage, there are still plenty of discoveries to be uncovered. It is now time to ask questions from another perspective. Confirming again the partner's desire for children is appropriate at this stage. Long-term career goals are also an important area to re-discuss. See if one of the partner's credit scores has changed. This is very important because after the marriage the couple may desire to purchase large items together such as a home or a vehicle. Some people may feel that it is shallow not to marry because of a person's credit history. But for a woman to know how hard she has worked to keep good credit and to make smart purchases to consider marrying someone who does not have the same sense of responsibility and focus can cause major resentment in a relationship. It can be the foundation of severe problems especially when bad financial choices continue throughout the duration of the marriage. It becomes unfair to the partner with solid credit because when buying joint purchases with him or her it brings the partner's credit rating down. It also becomes too rewarding for the partner with bad credit because he is riding on the favor of the other partner's good credit and he will never truly learn his lesson.

Consider premarital counseling during this phase. This can be done through your place of worship or with a marital counselor. Unfortunately, unless partners go to a church that requires premarital counseling before the actual ceremony, couples rarely schedule it. However, counseling before marriage can help determine and solve trouble issues before they actually happen. In many cases, it helps open discussion in areas that are either sensitive for the couple to discuss or that neither person thought of before the session. Couples who participate in premarital counseling tend to have more balance in their relationships and therefore less chance for outgrowth. Sometimes, counseling before marriage is the only time the man is required to consider his place, role and positioning in the relationship. Often he is asked hard questions such as: What is your vision for your family for the next five years? Does your soon-to-be wife agree with your vision? What is your personal plan for assuring that your family remains financially secure? When the man sees himself playing a major role in the successful financial well-being and overall vision for the family, it is less likely that the woman will feel overburdened and taken for granted. Most women don't mind tending to the home and contributing if their husbands see themselves as full partners. Even when a woman decides to or has to work outside the home, she is still less likely to be resentful if her husband is also doing his part.

Many women plan and dream their entire lives for their actual *wedding days*, although many people only envision the celebration, it is realistically just the beginning of the unknown.

Although for many couples the act of *sexual intimacy* usually begins in the liking stage, I believe it is very sacred and precious when it can be reserved until after the wedding. But due to the media and the societal pressure it is less and less popular to wait. When couples are willing to wait, it suggests to me that the partners have a great level of respect for one another and their bodies. It is a pure way to begin a lasting bond. In most cases, when a couple refrains from having premarital sex it is because of the religious beliefs of at least one of the mates. When the woman is the partner who wishes to refrain from premarital sex and she finds a mate who is willing to honor her commitment and refrain from having sex even though he does not necessarily agree, she has found a special mate, one who truly loves her mind, body and spirit.

One of the main reasons I feel it is very special to wait until after the marriage before becoming physically intimate is because *the act of sex should be the physical demonstration of the emotions developed through other stages.* If sex is exchanged during the like or dating stages, often not enough emotions have been secured to keep the relationship going after the sex. The focus becomes the sex because that is the strongest feeling that has been exchanged thus far. As mentioned previously, many times after sex women desire for the relationships to develop into something stronger because of the increased emotions that have developed through sex, but men often get consumed and caught up on the physical feelings of sex. *In many cases, after sex, the women start wanting more control and wanting to be exclusive, which may turn into desperation and the feeling of wanting more. For men, the physical pleasures of sex are likely to recede and they start wanting less.*

It is very easy to confuse sex and intimacy before marriage, because the couple is unlikely to feel the impact of being intimate without having sex. However, after marriage, this confusion is one of the main reasons why some women tend to feel imbalanced when it comes to their mates. Usually after children are born, when life becomes much more stressful, the woman needs her husband to understand that couples can be intimate without sex and she very much needs these acts of intimacy. For many women, intimacy means holding hands, opening doors or massaging their backs. Today, many women feel intimacy is also helping with laundry, putting away the dishes or helping the kids with homework.

The role of intimacy is definitely changing as the stress of life increases. *Acts of intimacy help prepare the woman to be dynamic inside of the bedroom.* Many times, if there is no intimacy beforehand the woman is unable to be mentally ready for fulfilling sex. She starts feeling that the sexual act is selfish and all about her husband. She begins to feel that if he really cared about her outside of having sex, he would be willing to help ease the load of household chores before they have sex. *Acts of intimacy say "I love you" and without it acts of sex say only "I want you."* After having children and coping with the stress of life, the wife often needs more from her husband, but many times she neglects to effectively communicate this to him. The only thing that he notices is that his wife is complaining that she needs more from him, but he neglects to ask what she really means.

After the wedding day and sexual intimacy, it is time to live out the promise of *marriage*—to execute what has been planned in the proposal stage. It is now time to work. It is not uncommon for people to feel shocked, saddened or simply strange soon after the wedding, because the thrill and the fun of planning the celebration are over. There has been so much excitement and hype on having a perfect wedding day that it is easy to feel like an old married couple when there is nothing to look forward to but the actual marriage itself.

Marriage allows partners to see what their mates really look like every morning. They learn real fast what they love most and what they don't like about their mates. Unfortunately, the things that a woman doesn't like about her mate are the very things that she is going to have to try and not focus on as she tries to be fair in her relationship. The things she loves the most will get little or no attention. In fact they might disappear all together. It will seem as if it will take twenty love thoughts to cover over one hate thought. That is why friendship is such an important mechanism in romantic relationships.

Many would agree that the emotion of love is a fragile, intense and unpredictable ground on which to solely base a marriage. Having a friendship with a spouse helps to relax and calm down the bad thoughts about him or her and it allows those feelings to be replaced by acceptance and understanding, because spouses care about their mates as people. It also helps partners not to pick apart and emphasize what they don't like about their spouses but instead gives them more of an understanding and emphasis on the things that makes each partner unique and different.

Marriage is not a time for shocking beginnings. It is a common trend for one of the mates to desire to undergo a drastic personal change after he or she says "I do." One to three years after marriage, it is not unusual for one of the mates to leave his or her job to embrace entrepreneurial opportunities, have a desire to go to school or make a large purchase exclusively for him or herself. When these changes have not been discussed prior to marriage, it can cause the other mate to question the true happiness of his or her spouse. It is also common for the mate who makes no changes to feel like he or she has been used or taken for granted so that the other partner can fulfill his or her dreams and move ahead with personal goals. The provider knows that the likelihood of the other spouse being able to make such a drastic change without the consistency of the provider's personal income would be impossible. Then the mate who makes no changes starts thinking of the dreams that he or she also wanted to pursue but allowed him or herself to forgo and forget about for the betterment of the couple. This is a very unfortunate way to begin a marriage; it usually creates a resentment that lasts through the duration of the relationship.

Lifetime discovery is the final phase in relationships. The foundation and authenticity of a relationship forms during this time. *In this phase a couple really learns together what they have and what they don't have.* They discover the strength of their love, the loyalty of their mates and the level of support during hardships. Partners truly learn the depth of their relationship. They find out that what they have either is something worth keeping or has dwindled in value.

During this stage, the love the couple once shared changes. The feelings of love that made partners giggle, blush or smile changes. *It transforms from a love that partners feel to a love of action.* One common mistake people make is that they expect the romantic, giggly love to continue through the duration of the relationship. When it doesn't, some people think either love has disappeared or their passion has been lost in the complexity of life. Many couples neglect to understand that love goes through different stages. Each stage of love is just as credible and significant as the others. When romantic love develops into a mature love and greater friendship, it requires the romance to be planned. It may not naturally appear as it did in early times. As life stressors increase, it will be more difficult to put romance in everyday life. Instead of living with the fact that the romantic love no longer exists, it is important that couples make conscious efforts to put it back in their relationships. This is the time to schedule date nights or surprise mates with special gifts or secret getaways. When couples are willing to put this extended effort into their marriages, it is a good sign that they will be together for a lifetime.

When He is Not Who He Says He Is

Donna had noticed Christopher for several weeks at the health spa she visited and she decided to make the first move for a potential date. So when Christopher responded positively by providing his phone number to her, she was pleasantly surprised. As Donna started to get to know Christopher on their first date, he was more than she could have ever imagined. He was a thirty-two-year-old information technology administrator for a multi-national corporation, earning a salary in excess of $82,000. He owned an upscale home in a private community and was also studying to become a recreational aircraft pilot. On their second date, Christopher took Donna to a nearby airport for a flying lesson. This date was followed by romantic dinners at chic restaurants, movies and evenings listening to jazz music. Christopher had a knack for introducing Donna to exciting new hobbies. At Donna's request, Christopher took her to a shooting range to learn to fire a 9mm automatic pistol. The couple had sex after only a few dates.

Later in the relationship Donna disclosed to Christopher that she was a thirty-six-year-old unemployed attorney who was an aspiring writer with three small children at home. She never revealed to Christopher that she had been receiving disability checks due to a nervous breakdown she had years before. She was afraid to disclose the real facts, because he was the most refreshing, ambitious and intelligent man she had ever met. Christopher often bragged about his net worth, investments and online trading activities, but Donna was quick to listen because she found him so interesting.

After only four months of dating things changed. The romantic dinners and movies abruptly ended. Christopher stopped returning Donna's calls and was never available when Donna called him on his cell phone. As Donna soon found out, not everything was as it appeared. Christopher's exclusive home was actually owned by him *and* his ex-girlfriend and was being sold due to their breakup. He was also facing a layoff from his prestigious IT position. Although he had spent almost four thousand dollars on flying lessons to obtain his pilot's license and talked of buying an airplane, when his car was totaled in an automobile accident, he could not afford to replace it. Donna was left to wonder if her dream man had intentionally misled her about his financial independence to gain intimacy.

Reaching Up
Most women are guilty of having daydreamed of ideal mates who are actually prince-like intellectually, socially and financially even if they themselves are lacking in education, looks and social skills. Yes, there are those few examples that we can all attest to where this becomes a reality in someone's life. But most people end up with someone who is either lower than their original expectations or someone who is comparable to their own levels.

The media is largely to blame for the unrealistic expectations in our society. The new fascination with reality shows supports that the core objective is to make an average person into an overnight sensation. This is true for television shows like *The Bachelor and American Idol* or game shows such as *Who Wants To Be A Millionaire?* and *Minute to Win It*. As a society we must ask ourselves if we are adopting a belief that we can have and become anything we desire without working for it—that fame and fortune will happen overnight. We read or view this happening to a very select few people and may believe it will and can happen in our lives too.

For many of us, even in our relationships we want the opposite of what we are, especially if we view aspects of ourselves negatively. If we were born poor and are poverty stricken, we think we deserve someone who was born into a privileged life. *In most cases, our relationship visions are more than what we can realistically expect.* Romantic dreams of the perfect mate are usually just that—dreams. The other person equally has dreams. Many people are looking for that certain someone who can make their lives more successful, creative or adventurous. Someone who can take them from the level at which they are presently and elevate them in areas they seek but have not found within themselves. Instead of looking to our own selves for success and wholeness, many of us desire for mates to raise us to this higher level and this is unfair.

Recall Donna, who definitely was guilty of having this overnight success mentality. Yes, she was an attorney, but she was out of work, had past mental instability and three small children at home. Many men would not be attracted to her due to the complexity of her circumstances. She watched Christopher for some time before she approached him. She noticed the type of car he drove, the clothes he wore and how he carried himself overall. She could tell from his mere presence that there was a good chance that he was someone who could "add to her life" because of what he had to offer.

She dreamed of someone who could rescue her from her present situation. She revealed little of her personal background to Christopher initially. She left out the fact that she was an unemployed attorney with three small children until after they had developed a relationship. He thought she was a young, beautiful single woman when he first took her to fine restaurants and gave her flying lessons. Surely she knew that he would one day find out the truth and find out the complexities of her life and the past skeletons in her closet. It's easy to understand why she saw him as a fixer for her present situation. She wanted to gain personally from his money, his adventurous life and his success. He would have to help raise three children of whom he was not the biological father and deal with a woman with mental issues who was also unemployed. I believe Donna's unrealistic expectations positioned her to gain everything and for Christopher to not gain anything but problems. Whenever a relationship starts out with this type of imbalance, it is unlikely the relationship will develop into a lifetime of happiness and contentment.

Realistically, if Donna sought a man who was closer to her level financially and socially, possibly the relationship would have had a better chance of survival. Maybe she would not have been so embarrassed by her past hardships and would have felt comfortable sharing her problems, complexities and mishaps. When you find someone who is closer to your own status, he or she is also less likely to judge and be turned off by your background.

When Sex Can Ruin Your Relationship

Like many women, Donna felt that it was safe to have sex with Christopher when the opportunity presented itself. Since he had shown some initial interest by wining and dining her, she felt that the obvious next step in their relationship was sex; she felt that she owed him at least that. Women often assume that men expect sex and then they feel a sense of obligation because the men have been nice.

In the story of Donna and Christopher, we see Christopher as the person who has committed fraud in the relationship. More time was spent disclosing the details of his life before he started dating Donna versus after the intimacy happened. Within just four months, Christopher went from earning $82,000 per year and living in a quarter of a million dollar home to having to live with his ex-girlfriend.

Did Christopher commit relationship fraud or not? As Donna stated, it is difficult to tell if it was actually a conscious fraud that she experienced or if she was just the victim of bad timing. Donna is the one who approached Christopher, pursued him and asked him for his phone number; she had noticed him from afar for a while before she actually approached him at the gym. More than likely, if she noticed him, he also noticed her. He had every opportunity to make the first move. Because she approached him first, it is very unlikely that he developed such an outlandish lie about his salary and finances so quickly and for a woman whom he did not even approach. She was smitten with him first, not the other way around. Christopher had nothing to protect and no reason to try and impress, because he was the one being pursued.

Donna, on the other hand, had a reason to try and hide her present life circumstances. When you are trying to look attractive and desirable to a possible mate, you want your life status to seem as appetizing as possible. The story reveals that it was not until later in the relationship that Donna revealed the truth about her life and even then she did not tell the entire truth. In reality it was Donna who had the reason to lie and to fabricate a story, because she wanted to impress Christopher. *The one who is the most smitten is always the one who is the most vulnerable.*

It is not clear if Christopher was guilty of relationship fraud or not, but it is quite evident that Donna had a few tricks of her own.

6

The Secret Rewards of Outgrowing Him

It is a dangerous phenomenon when a wife feels that she has outgrown her husband based solely on the fact that she has gotten bored with him. It is especially serious when she is able to label and identify the areas in which she feels she has matured more. When a woman has put so much thought into the problem that she has actually given it a name, it suggests that she has put too much focus and energy into the downfall of her relationship and that perhaps she is over-thinking and overanalyzing the negative aspects that have impacted her relationship with her husband.

Pamela was married to Rodney for twenty-one years. Although Pamela made more money than Rodney, the couple worked for two decades to establish a middle-class lifestyle. They owned a nice home, did not have children and were financially secure. Pamela and Rodney could afford to take at least two vacations each year, sometimes to far-off places such as Aruba, Fiji and Italy. When they weren't vacationing together, they spent time with family or friends, attended concerts, went on shopping trips and went to the theatre.

Pamela, however, became bored with Rodney. She believed she had begun to outgrow him for several years, both intellectually and emotionally. Pamela complained that she was tired of doing the same old things. She said Rodney had lost his sense of adventure and interest in new things. Pamela caught the eye of a younger male co-worker and she filed for divorce in spite of Rodney's desire to stay married. She moved out of their home to an apartment, enjoying her new freedom and new love interest.

However, a year after the divorce, Pamela found herself alone. Her love interest had moved on and she was left to consider whether her once settled and predictable life of security with Rodney was as bad as she had thought. Meanwhile, Rodney had begun seeing another woman. Pamela realized that she might have moved too quickly in deciding that her old relationship was not worth keeping and she wished she had the stability of Rodney's boring personality again.

This true story is a sad one. For Pamela and Rodney to have worked so hard together to maintain a comfortable middle-class lifestyle and to have so many benefits, such as vacationing on a consistent basis, is a luxury that many couples never have. Based on the story they told me, their lifestyle seemed stable and predictable and many would consider their relationship a success. The scenario tells nothing about infidelity, abuse or a lack of respect for each other. However, Pamela, after twenty-one years of marriage, looked at Rodney and decided she was bored with him and that he was not as fun as he used to be. She believed she had outgrown him intellectually. I wonder if Pamela was not confusing intelligence with energy of life. Nothing in the story suggests that she was more intelligent than Rodney, even though she is a school teacher and he is a baker at a local bakery. It is true she is college educated and he is not, but she knew this long before she decided to marry him.

Pamela and Rodney were in the lifetime discovery phase of their relationship. As discussed previously, it is imperative in this stage that couples learn not to rely on the romantic love feelings that they once had, but to create a more mature love and friendship. Spouses have to learn to create the romance in their relationship all over again. They should not assume that their feelings will remain as before; they have to work hard to create more mature love relationships.

Pamela's hasty decision to leave her marriage and a husband whom she had grown to know and trust was not wise. For her to think that her relationship with a younger man would prove to give her more long-term contentment than her twenty-one-year-old marriage was not good judgment. Boredom is a small issue to fix. It is a shame not to work hard to do so. Pamela had been married so long that she took for granted what it means to be committed and to have someone who was there only for her. When her new love interest proved fleeting and unreliable, she realized that Rodney had steadfast qualities she hadn't appreciated. The energy and time that Pamela put into creating the excitement that she experienced with her one-year fling could have been put into developing more romance in her marriage.

When she tried to reconcile with Rodney, Pamela was very surprised that he had found someone else. *She never thought that another woman, maybe even one who had more to offer, would actually want her ex-husband.* Pamela remembered when he begged her not to end the relationship. She had assumed that Rodney would be at home waiting for her to return. Once she learned that he had moved on, he looked even more desirable. She knew then that she had made a mistake.

There is an important lesson to be learned from Pamela's experience. When thinking about leaving a relationship that has not caused emotional or physical abuse, ask these questions: Would the relationship still be worth leaving if you knew that you might never be in a committed marriage again with someone else? What if you decide you want to go back but your spouse has moved on with someone else? Is it still worth leaving? *If you know in your heart that you would prefer to be alone than to be married, even if your spouse remarries, you are at least thinking about the worst-case scenario before ending your marriage.* Many people leave their marriages believing that they will soon replace the relationships. However, the likelihood of a second marriage, especially for women, is becoming more improbable, so partners need to think carefully about whether they should work harder on their current marriages. *If you consider the worst-case scenario and still can say yes to leaving, you are no longer emotionally attached to your present relationship.*

It is so easy and common for people to focus on what is wrong in their lives that it is rare that they appreciate the aspects that are going right. They tend to magnify the things that are wrong so much until they are all they see. The reality is that if partners are concerned with the imbalance in their relationships, it appears that everything in life is a mess. Spouses become disgusted with their jobs outside the home, the kids seem extra agitated and the house appears to be unusually dirty. When one thing goes bad it seems that everything goes bad.

Power Gained When You Have Outgrown Him

Although women are the main ones who become growingly agitated with the imbalance in their relationships, the other side of the untold story is that these same women *gain the reward of an enormous amount of personal power through imbalance.* No decisions are made without their approvals. The households would stop functioning without them. It can be a turnoff for women when men have a strong sense of need and dependence on them. *Although this power becomes draining and stressful, there is also an incredible personal high and sense of control that comes with it.* It is a rewarding feeling to know that the world keeps turning simply because you are living in it. There is a sense of loyalty and indebtedness that he also feels toward her that can be a payoff. The more imbalances there are in a relationship, the more loyalty women tend to get from their dependent husbands. *The problem is that as relationships progress women want their husbands to be loyal not because they need them but instead because they love them.*

The second reward to which most women would never confess is the personal control over the husband that comes when there is imbalance. The more severe the imbalance is, the less confident he becomes and the more confident she becomes. His lack of confidence and *need* for his wife causes him to stay in the relationship when he would normally leave. He does whatever he can to avoid arguments in fear of where they would lead, so he communicates less or tends to agree with his wife when they do argue. The wife also talks less because she finds less need to include her husband in decisions and everyday life since she does everything anyway. The spouses find that they are growing further and further apart. The wife knows she can make it financially and emotionally on her own, because she feels like she is alone already.

There is power in a wife's knowing that the household runs because of her vision, energy and actions. If she had concerns before about her ability to conquer and achieve, these now are gone. Although she complains about having no help and having all the control, most women are not quick to give it up.

To finally get help and more balance from her husband means to share in the power and control and women who believe they have outgrown their husbands don't want to do that. If the control had been shared from the very beginning, most women would find it more acceptable. But to have had the taste of all of that power for years and then to have to share it with their husbands is something that some women are not willing to do.

Although it is not a topic that husbands choose to discuss, many men may be aware that they're not doing what they should. Although it may seem like the husband is totally irresponsible, his confidence level is deeply suffering. He realizes that the children respond to him differently than to his wife. It hurts him that that they come to him as the very last resort, because they know that their mom is the true decision maker. He notices that his wife is becoming more and more independent. He understands less and less of her personal world. When he thinks about the possibility of them separating one day, he secretly wonders if he will be able to survive alone. He knows that he will have to balance the checkbook, cook for himself and pay the bills on time. Because he is so accustomed to his wife handling these everyday tasks, he wonders how good he will be at them. Though earlier he didn't realize it, he has become very dependent on his wife taking care of things. He knows that she will be able to move on, but he realizes that if they broke up, he would need to find another woman who could also take care of everyday things.

The Break-Up, a movie with Jennifer Aniston playing the role of Brooke and Vince Vaughn playing Gary, is about a couple that have definite imbalances in their relationship. It is a good illustration of what happens when a woman feels that she has outgrown her mate. Brooke works for an exclusive art firm in the city and Gary works with his brothers at a family tour guide business. They have a nice apartment in the city and seem to be doing well. The breakdown starts when Brooke arranges for friends to come over and Gary is consumed with his own agenda of playing videos games and relaxing after work. Brooke fusses about how tired she is and how she worked all day, fixed dinner, cooked for the company and entertained the guests all night and all she wants is for Gary to respect her enough to help with the dishes.

After going back and forth, Gary eventually decides that the video games can wait and that he will help Brooke with the dishes. When Brooke notices how reluctant and upset he is about this, she decides that she does not want his help and that she will do the dishes herself. The argument escalates and hateful words are exchanged. Brooke finally says that she is finished and cannot go any further with the relationship.

Brooke complains of wanting to feel appreciated and Gary wants to relax and not feel nagged when he comes home from work; this alone is the core of the relationship destruction. When it is time to move out, Gary tries to reconcile and admits that things got out of hand, but Brooke tells him that she is tired and that she does not have the energy to try again at the relationship.

Although *The Break-Up* was promoted as a romantic comedy, Brooke and Gary's relationship is not very funny and many of their problems are similar to those of real-life couples who are unhappy.[1]

Could a Wife be Jealous of Her Husband?

"Is it really that bad anyway?" is not an easy question and one that requires much soul searching. It is complex because if women allowed themselves to be honest, many times they are filled with jealousy when it comes to their husbands' lifestyles. Women see partners living on the good graces of their hard work and women are often envious of how easy their husbands' lives seem.

Beautiful and well-mannered children, clean homes, home-cooked meals and beautiful holiday celebrations are mostly due to what women have contributed. This especially holds true when there are financial imbalances. When the woman feels she has outgrown her husband intellectually, emotionally and also financially, there is little room for empathy and compassion. She begins to think more about her husband's casual life verses her uptight life that leaves her scrambling for time to herself.

She notices how hearty and authentic his laugh is during funny situations or television programs. She remembers when she was just as carefree, but now it is a rare opportunity for her to sit down and casually look at any television show, let alone a funny one.

The truth is, women could use a little of their partners' casualness and, in many cases, men could use a little focus on the overall concerns of the family. Women need some of their mates' attitudes toward life and they definitely need some of women's sense of responsibility. If both partners could mix their extremes, one major issue of the imbalance problem would be solved. Many women tend to be quite uptight and tense and therefore no fun to be around. But if they could learn to laugh often and be more lighthearted, women might find that the world, including the imbalances of their main relationships, is not so bad.

When women compare their lives to their husbands', it is worth asking, "Is it that bad anyway?" Although women often complain about the casualness of their husbands' lives versus the stressfulness of their own, I doubt it if women really want mates with the same amount of intensity. If mates worried and lived uptight existences that were comparable to women's, ladies would probably complain that they need to loosen up and relax. For many women, it is a turnoff to have a man who takes on the feminine characteristics of worry, stress and depression. Women so easily pinpoint this sense of unhappiness to the imbalance. However, at least they know that their partners bring some balance, because they are the opposite of their women. Some women have developed such strong personas that they are not able to tolerate worrisome men. They view it as being weak or too sensitive and see his emotions as feelings that challenge his personal manhood.

If the husband is honest about what he can contribute, is not threatened by what his wife brings to the relationship and is not afraid to communicate, she would learn to respect him for being open and honest.

If the wife focuses on what the husband does bring to the relationship verses what he doesn't, learns to capitalize and use her abilities to help uphold the family and gives her husband praise and support for what he does do right, perhaps her husband would learn to open up and trust her by revealing his true self for the first time or again.

From a more practical sense, *the husband's casualness and the wife's stress may cause imbalance for the couple, but in many cases it helps create a great sense of harmony for the children.* Children don't need two parents exactly the same. Since, in most cases, the wife has grown into a no-nonsense powerhouse, it would really be a reason for concern if the husband was just as fast-thinking, fast-talking and overwhelmed. The children would feel as though they were being raised by the military instead of by two parents who love them. It would be detrimental in the long-term if both parents had the tendency to be carefree and casual without giving a strong sense of direction. If balance can be achieved with both parents living in their extremes, it really can become a perfect union. What one parent could not do the other parent would be well-equipped in achieving. Each parent having their own specific roles, while being respected by each other, could be the perfect balance.

7

Secrets Your Mother Did Not Tell You

Let me share some secrets about self and relationships, unraveling some truths that may confirm what you already know or shock you completely. These are truths that everyone should know when involved in a long-term or serious relationship.

Women Can Be Nags

Yes I said it and yes I mean it. Women have the tendency to nag. Women hate being ignored and they think quick and act quick. They want a reaction quickly and are looking for a profound response. Many women tend to get inpatient and want their husbands to think and act just as quickly as they do, but it likely will never happen. Women tend to be multitaskers, but being able to do multiple things at one time is a blessing and also a curse. Women get frustrated when their husbands can't multitask as well as they can. *In many cases, men can only do one thing at a time and think and move slower than women.* This

This can bring out the very worst in women, because they want their husbands to act and be like women.

Unlike women, men have an innate need to want to "fix it." They want to feel that they can solve problems for women and this gives them purpose and meaning. Now, they may not fix it on women's timetables or they may not fix it the way women want it, but "fixing it" is their blessing to their wives.

Thought: *Don't expect your man to think, move or react like he is a woman because he is not.*

Too Many Men Opt for the Silent Approach

Too many men neglect to speak up when they need to. This lack of confrontation or communication often stems from issues from childhood.

Let's return to our discussion on mothers who prefer loving their sons instead of teaching them. For example, many times a mother speaks to the coach on her son's behalf or calls the teacher to ask important questions about homework instead of teaching the son to be responsible for himself. Too often young boys never learn the skills of communicating, asking questions and ultimately getting what they need done on their own. These young boys grow up to be young men who still lack the ability to confront appropriately and negotiate properly. So when it is time for a "mama's boy" to speak up to his mother and tell her to respect his relationship or when his wife needs her husband to discuss their son's behavioral problems with the school principal, too often the husband is directionless about where to begin and he is not equipped or confident enough to address the problems at hand.

After a while, the wife finds it easier to solve the problems herself and she stops counting on her husband. This increases her resentment toward him and decreases her need for him.

Even when they are together he will often allow her to speak up and be confrontational because he has learned that she can do it better, faster and more effectively. She thinks fast, knows what she wants and has the confidence to execute it. Although the lack of ability to communicate deflates his male ego and can often embarrass him, the husband often never learns the skills needed to stand up and be the assertive man he can be. Deep down he knows that he should be able to effectively speak up, but his unease in this area deflates his manhood and causes him to question himself.

In too many situations, what triggers a man to communicate is anger. It is then and only then does everything that his feelings are expressed. This inability to communicate affects his relationships. Once he marries, he doesn't develop insight into what his wife is feeling and finds that he is not as comfortable as he should be communicating with his own children.

Thought: *If you are in a relationship with a man who is not comfortable with serious communication or confrontation, realize that this skill was probably never taught to him. Just as you want more from him, he also wants more from himself in this area. Your level of frustration does not match the deep feeling of embarrassment that he has concerning his discomfort with communicating feelings.*

Speak Up or Lose Your "Right" to Complain

Ask, ask and then ask again. *If you don't speak up then you lose your right to complain now and later.* Oftentimes women expect their partners to read their minds. They get upset and angry when partners don't know automatically what they need, want or are thinking. Women expect that because their partners have known them for so long that they should know what they want, when they want it and how to go about getting it.

We can't read our spouses' minds. But if we could, we would be a lot less confused and frustrated in our relationships with them. If we don't ask for what we want, in a marriage and also in our careers, most times we are not going to get it.

People in our lives expect us to speak up when there is something wrong. We expect others to tell us what they want or need and we should return the favor. It is not only unfair, it is also arrogant to assume that people know us so much and have us so exclusively on their minds that they will automatically know what we want and when we want it.

Thought: *Women are complex beings. They are hard to understand and have the tendency to dissect a situation. Many women don't realize their spouses don't have a clue on how to please them.*

Hold On Loosely

With everything in life, every facet, every career move and every relationship, it is best to hold on loosely. If you hold on too tightly whatever you are holding on to may bring you anxiety, desperateness and sorrow. For example, if a woman holds on too tight to her children they probably will disappoint her, because they will fight to grow up while she is trying to keep them close. When a person holds on too tight to her job, she will be anxious due to the fact that she is creating a standard much too high for her to ever meet. Whether you are dating or married, hold on loosely to what you have. When your mate disappoints, you will avoid being devastated because all along you knew that he was merely human.

Thought: *When you have the ability to hold on loosely you will have the tendency to be more attractive. This is one of the reasons why good girls like bad boys—because bad boys have the tendency to hold on loosely. We are always attracted to those who look like they have places to go.*

Your Relationship is Not Your Family's Business

Too many women discuss their problems, sex lives and overall conditions of their relationships with their friends and families. When friends ask how things are going in a relationship, a vague answer is the most appropriate: "Everything is okay" is enough of a response.

When you disclose negative secrets about your relationship to your loved ones, it is unfair to your mate. Because your family and friends love you, they are going to be on your side and view your mate negatively when things aren't going well. It can ruin a relationship when a mate feels that you can't be around your family without discussing him. He needs to feel that he can trust you with both the good and the bad of the relationship without allowing yourself to be influenced by others.

If a woman needs support to cheer her on in the middle of the relationship, this might be a sign of lack of maturity and preparedness for a serious relationship. Much too often women want their loved ones to take their sides when arguing with spouses and then they want loved ones also to be ready to forgive and forget at the same time that they do. This is simply not realistic. What a woman tells her loved ones and the negative behavior she shares about her husband clouds her loved ones' opinions about him, possibly throughout the duration of the relationship.

Thought: *Don't say things in private about your mate that you don't want revealed in public.*

We Teach People How To Treat Us

Every day and in every relationship, we teach others how to treat us by what we accept from them. If we accept bad behavior it is our issue, because we have allowed it to happen to us. Although it would be nice, it is not solely up to other people to make sure they are kind, considerate and treating us with boundless respect. It is instead our responsibility to make sure that we only allow respectful people into our circles of friends. When we don't speak up we teach them that what they are doing is okay. This is especially true of our mates. It is not up to our mates to read our minds or determine for us what is okay and not okay.

Too often in a relationship we will go on for months and possibly years never speaking up about negative behavior. Although we don't like what the other person is doing and we might make the mistake of telling others about what he is doing wrong, we rarely tell our mates. Many times they are the last to know. We allow the bad behavior to become part of our lives and part of our relationships. Then when we are overwhelmed by the behavior and other stressors in our lives we have the tendency to get angry.

We explode our anger about a behavior that they have been doing all along. This sudden angry reaction will often catch our mates by surprise, because they had no idea that their behavior was a problem since we have allowed it to go on for so long.

Thought: *People will treat you the way that you allow them to.*

You Will Never Get More Than What You Ask

If the asking price for your car is $10,000 the potential buyer is not going to offer you $15,000. *You will never get more than what you ask.* The same goes for relationships. If you only ask your spouse to dry the dishes, he probably will not also volunteer to sweep the floor.

Thought: *Be sure that the bare minimum of what you ask for is enough for you, even if your situation never gets any better or easier. Make certain you are more than satisfied with what you are either asking or accepting, because getting more than what you have asked for is very unlikely.*

Your Power is Not What Attracts Him

Women have a complex role to play. They must be tough and nurturing at the same time. Women have also learned that they tend to move up the corporate ladder more quickly when they show less of an emotional side at work. Needing to change and adapt behavior based on environment can be difficult and confusing. Although men are not generally interested in women being wimpy, most men do appreciate women who are comfortable exerting their feminine qualities.

Men are very turned on by a confident woman. *Confident* does not mean unapproachable or arrogant. It simply means that a woman feels she has everything already in her to live to her greatest potential. But men also appreciate a woman who is not afraid to show her softer side and ask for help.

Thought: *A man needs to feel that he has a purpose and a role. If he gets the idea that a woman can do everything for herself, then he will be turned off, because it will be obvious that there is no room for him in her life.*

Never Invest More than What You Can Afford to Lose

Many people expend too much energy, focus and love on other people who are not worthy and then they have nothing left for the more important relationships in their lives, including themselves. Never invest more in a relationship than you can afford to lose. Don't give all your time away when you don't have a lot of time to give. In a more practical sense, don't stay up all night talking on the phone when you have problems getting up early for work. *Only give what you've got then hold back a little for yourself.* More than likely, if you are giving more than what you can actually afford to, the other person is not giving back equally to you.

Thought: *You don't have an unlimited amount of energy, time and tolerance. You do have a breaking point and trying to please your mate is not worth depleting all your resources and unconditional love. Evaluate the person's worth and then cautiously give the level of his value.*

If You Liked Yourself More You Would Like Him Less

It is hard to know how you really feel about another person when you don't like yourself very much. When battling with self-esteem issues most everyone seems better and more worthy. Ironically, until you have a healthy level of confidence you really don't know how you feel about someone else, because you are looking at the world through a "low confidence" lens.

When confidence is low we tend to settle, because deep down we don't feel worthy to be in a relationship anyway. We become grateful that others want to spend time with us and we tend to compromise our values because we are desperate for companionship.

It is important to understand that "not liking yourself" can stem from various causes, but our discussion will focus on the top three. One of the most common is that we are often uncomfortable with our physical looks. We have an unrealistic perspective when we compare ourselves to celebrities in the media. They are not only thin, but beautiful as well. It takes a healthy self-esteem to truly like yourself when you are simply normal in this world of competition.

As a coach I have found many of my clients are in desperate states because they feel that they are high maintenance and unlikeable people. They tend to be critical and unpleasant. Because they know they are overdramatic, they end up settling for mates they don't really desire because they know that they are difficult to love. For instance, when you feel that your mate is gorgeous and has the opportunity to date women more attractive than you, it often can cause self doubt, blame and jealousy. In this case, if you liked yourself more you would not be so smitten with your mate and it would drastically decrease your level of desperateness. This same thing can easily happen when you feel that you are not as successful as your partner.

Thought: *If you liked yourself more you would like him less and because of your newfound confidence he would end up liking you more.*

Forgive Others for Your Sake

We have all been guilty of holding on to resentment and anger in situations less onerous than these emotions actually deserve. Many of us also have held innocent people hostage because of how other people have wrongly treated their mates in past relationships. Although it is always difficult to be hurt by others, when we recognize that people have flaws, we are more likely to be able to forgive, let go, forget and walk away.

Forgiveness is about you; it is not about them. Oftentimes when we hold onto anger and hurt, the person who actually did the hurting is not even thinking about us. All of the energy and thought consumption we put into being hurt and angry is wasted on someone who is not worth it. When we hold on to anger it affects our sleep patterns and our trust in other people and it consumes our thoughts when we should be thinking about people and things that are worthy of our energy.

Thought: *Forgive because you realize that you expected too much from the other person and that he is simply human. Forgive because you realize that the person or situation is not worthy of the energy that you are giving it. Forgive because you have more valuable people in your life who deserve your attention right now. Forgive because you realize that although you may be obsessed with the other person he is not consumed with thoughts about you.*

When People Show You Who They Are Believe Them

If we could acknowledge what we can physically see many of us would be in much better places emotionally. Early in a relationship you see signs of who the other person really is. The signs are in how the person treats other people, how he handles anger and the level of respect and admiration other people give him. If we would just learn to see what is right before us instead of ignoring the obvious we would be in a better place.

Many times, it is so easy for us to speak truth and wisdom in a friend's life. We can spot a "no good dog" miles away when we are not personally involved with him. But when we are trying to figure out our own circumstances we tend to use blinders. Our vision and perspective becomes unclear and unfocused. You can't keep someone who doesn't want to be kept, you can't rescue someone who doesn't want to be rescued and you can't save someone who doesn't want to be saved.

Thought: *You can't base people's maturity level on their biological ages; you must base it on the way they treat you and others.*

Stop Lying to Yourself

"I don't need a man anyway." We are hearing this phrase more and more. Maybe this phrase has some truth to it. Possibly a person doesn't need a significant other, but many definitely want one. Saying that you don't need a man is another form of control. It is easier to shut out that part of your life so that you will be less likely to be hurt or disappointed again.

It is very dangerous to *need* a man. Not only is it unhealthy to need him but he also doesn't want you to need him in that manner. Your partner wants to feel that you are involved with him because you want to be, not because you need to be. When your mate starts feeling needed more than wanted it is easy for him to feel used and taken for granted.

Thought: *It is a strong and confident woman who can admit that although she can live happily alone she would prefer to have a husband who loves and admires her. Lying to yourself and stating that you don't care just shows your discomfort in this area.*

8

Deadly Mistakes Women Make

Making a Man Your One and All

Some women tend to forget that they lived successfully before their spouses and still have the ability to live successfully without them. Once started on the marital path many women feel almost incomplete and unsatisfied unless their husbands are with them on each endeavor and interest. The most important mission in their lives becomes to be and stay married. They feel this defines and completes how successful they have been with their lives.

Too often women lose all other ambitions and forget about the love and support of the rest of their family and friends. Their husbands then become primarily what they care about. Too many times and much too often satisfying her husband becomes a woman's sole purpose. He becomes her complete everything until she become so resentful that his actions are not perfect but instead flawed. Her love turns to anger and her anger turns to hate. Allowing one person to have such an importance in life is unwise and also unfair both to him and the woman. No man could ever satisfy all of the expectations and the perfectionist attributes that his spouse is expecting from him, because he is human and imperfect.

Why does love have such power and control in our lives? One of the reasons is because the emotion of love comes with almost every imaginable feeling. Love includes passion, lust, obsession, anger, hate and excitement, to name a few concomitant emotions. The word *love* takes us on an emotional ride and it brings along with it every emotion available to us.

Women may become obsessed because what they expected from their relationships falls short of the exalted ideal painted in their minds.

Positioning Yourself as the Giver

As we discussed earlier, in a premarital relationship and later in the marriage itself, one of the most dangerous mistakes women can make is to position themselves solely as givers instead of receivers. This causes the relationship to become imbalanced. If a woman doesn't have a need for her husband to do anything for her then he will not do anything for her. If she undertakes fulfilling every task and taking on each burden and every function and is willing to take on the full responsibility of the relationship, she has completely displaced any need for him. As time goes on and marital as well as family obligations grow, he has no significant purpose or meaning in the relationship.

Not Counting Your Blessings

We must look around us and count the blessings that we currently have. There is such power, harmony and wisdom in simply being satisfied with where you are in life and what you presently have. When you are always looking for the next thrill, the next level or the next surprise in your life then it is hard to be completely grateful and live in the moment right now. This same perspective is also important in marriage.

When I was teaching at a university, a very attractive woman, Dora, was getting her bachelor's degree in nursing. She was in her forties and a non-traditional student. She had a nine-year-old son, but had never been married. After class one day I noticed that she seemed depressed and I casually asked her if everything was okay. As if a valve had opened, she poured out her feelings of loneliness and pain. She said that she wanted to get married and share her life with someone but there were absolutely no prospects for her. She went on to reveal that not only was she not seriously dating, but also she had not had a serious boyfriend for over five years. She mentioned that she felt guilty being so depressed, because everything else in her life was fine. She had a great job, a wonderful son, a beautiful support team of friends and family and no strong concerns or problems in any other area in her life. She knew that her concern with marriage was affecting her studies, her job and interfering with her interaction with her son.

There is healing, self renewal and wisdom in simply "being well"—that is, feeling satisfied with where you are in life and no longer wondering, fretting or even focusing on what you don't have in your life. That evening, I looked searchingly at Dora and asked, "Dora, if you never get blessed with a husband do you think you can find it within yourself to give the entire idea of marriage a rest, take what you have in your life right now and simply be well with it?" She looked back at me and seemed somewhat shocked so I continued to explain, "Are you able to look at all of the blessings you currently have in your life and accept them and just be satisfied? *Because right now all of the beautiful things that you have going for yourself and the many things that you have been given that other people can only wish for are being discounted, drowned out by your desire for a husband.*" I tried to explain that one of the wisest things that she could do was to "get well" with her present circumstance. To stop worrying and obsessing. When she did this, she would become the person who would begin to attract the type of man that she was looking for. I explained that she was simply too desperate and the idea of marriage was too important to her to be successful in it. If she was to get married at that point, she would have had the tendency to hold on too tightly to the marriage in fear of losing what she had. This would have caused anxiety and fear within herself and her husband to tend to distance himself. I concluded that she needed to first work on herself in this area and to "become well with it." If she could see herself as a complete person without a man, she would find a suitable companion or he would find her.

Does He Love You More?

Many women don't like it when I ask them this question, because it causes them to become too real with their feelings. When I ask men, "Do you believe that the man should love the woman more?" about 85 percent of them believe that they should. *Most men know that they should love women more but women don't know this.* My husband and male clients have taught me that the only way to create balance in a relationship is if the man actually loves the woman more.

I am a firm believer that what is wrong with many relationships today is that women love men more than men love them. When this happens things are completely unbalanced. In many cases, when a man falls in love he usually falls in love quickly. If it takes him months and months to fall in love with a woman, he may say he loves her but many times he is not in love with her.

My husband provided an interesting explanation from a man's point of view that the reason there is such a need for the man to love the woman more is because a woman is designed to give everything she has in her relationships. Even looking back at how our mothers and grandmothers worked, labored and suffered over the well-being of the family, it is undeniably one of the greatest expressions of love that most of us have seen. Although the father loves deeply as well, it is a different type of love and a different type of depth that comes from the mother. Her ability to give her heart, soul and mind to her family over and over again and to each individual child is simply amazing; she is designed this way. So even if the husband and the wife loved each other the same, when the wife starts unconditionally giving to her family, the energy she put in the relationship becomes grossly unbalanced from the energy that he is designed to give.

My husband went on to explain that when a man is more in love with the woman than she is with him, as she gives her heart, soul and mind to her family he will take up the slack in other places in her life, to make sure she is nourished in other areas. He will help out more in the house, be consistently concerned with her well–being and try to balance the other areas of her life with love so that she is not so exhausted, tired and overwhelmed with being a mother and wife; he will do these things simply because he loves her.

This does not mean that the man should be completely focused on his wife and the woman should not be interested in him. In fact, I have had clients who consider their husbands' total focus on and unconditional love for them as signs of weakness. They completely discount the "authenticity" of their husbands' love and criticize them for it. In such cases the woman takes for granted her husband's graciousness and some may even become verbally and physically abusive. Too many times she will start looking for a "bad boy" whom she has to fight to keep. The fight and the challenge, unfortunately, becomes a turn-on for some women, however. I believe just like the man, the woman has a responsibility to love, honor and respect her spouse.

When we talk about how to prevent the phenomena of women outgrowing their mates, a lot can be accomplished through the men having more love for their wives. When a son witnesses his father consistently taking special care of his mother, it establishes a natural standard in the son to do the same thing in his future relationships. *As I mentioned previously, the most influential parent in a child's life is the same sex parent.* When the son clearly sees his father as the giver and his mother as the receiver, he begins to see his own role differently.

This is similar for a young woman looking at the relationship between her father and her mother. It is imperative that she witness and understand a positive relationship between a man and a woman. If she sees this when growing up, the daughter understands the preciousness of her father's respect for her mother. She notices how her parents are different and more loving than friends' parents and starts to appreciate the harmony in her home. She admires that her mother is still strong, successful and capable in practicing the art of being a woman without denying the strength already established in her. The daughter creates a mindset about relationships and about what is right and wrong with them. She becomes more selective in what she wants for herself because of what she has learned from her parents.

Of course, there will always be problems, arguments and disagreements in any relationship. However, if a "good" wife recognizes that her husband is doing the very best that he can, she will be less likely to feel taken for granted. He will have a natural way of trying to create balance for her, simply because he cares and loves her more.

9

Prince Charming Doesn't Exist

The lie for women begins early in life. It starts with the same fairy tale story that enters our world when we are very young and impressionable. The love fairy tales have the same underlying message—one that we don't seem to be able to escape. Just to name a few: *Cinderella, Snow White and the Seven Dwarfs, The Little Mermaid* and *The Princess and the Frog*, recently made into an animated feature film; they all began and end the same way.

As a society we never seem to grow tired of the same storyline that created the plot for all of the fairy tales. *The fairy tales are similar and set up the standards for what we deem to be perfect relationships.* All have predictable messages that we have grown to know, yet there is no complaint or other expectation that society verbalizes about the love in fairy tales. They all begin by telling of an unfortunate, innocent and simple girl who has been mistreated in life. The story always lays out how hard her life has been and then vastly improves after she grows up, meets and marries a handsome, rich and charming prince. Out of all of the other females in the town the prince seems to always choose the female who has the most humble beginning and the one who seems the least likely to be picked. In all the fairy tales we have grown to admire, the other women in the town gasp at the thought of being with Mr. Perfect. They would do anything to marry him and they also have a hope that he will choose them. Although women end up settling for a more realistic lifestyle with their own husbands, the fairy tales show a desperation in their eyes despite the fact that they are "not princess material themselves" nor have any shame or embarrassment in wanting the prince for themselves.

We start reading fairy tales to young daughters so they will have "sweet dreams" at night. Although as parents we know that the story is just a fictional tale, the little girls listening to the story start believing the message behind the tradition. That dream of living happily ever after with a Prince Charming often becomes an unspoken hope as daughters grow. This tradition is supported by films, video games and toys, which have been created to merchandise fairy tales, making them even more alive and creating a realistic image of something that is unrealistic. Although little girls grow up and become educated women who undertake careers and create adult lives, there is an unspoken belief and hope that there is a real life prince out there for every woman. Although things are different now and most women don't make a career out of trying to be perfect or just right for their mates, that underlying message about being rescued by Prince Charming formed when women were young and impressionable never really leaves them. Until recently, many parents also believed that one day their daughters would be swept off their feet by handsome princes. Now parents wonder if their daughters will ever get married and settle down. Today the words *old maid* are no longer heard as often, but the stigma of that lifestyle still quietly exists. Because it is still such a rarity to marry for the first time when a woman is in her forties and fifties, we tend to be just a little embarrassed for women at this point in their lives still searching for that elusive perfect match.

Although some women opt for single lives, for most women there still is a hope and a belief that maybe, just maybe, Mr. Right will magically appear and turn their entire futures completely around. *The expression of hope begins to change as women grow older and the strength of their hope greatly lessens over time. Could one reason why women tend to be so unsatisfied with their men be because they are so different than the Prince Charming women learned to believe in?*

The Tarnished Prince
I feel one thing that is not usually spoken of that is wrong with this fairy tale ideal is the unfairness it silently places on men. All of the expectations are placed on the man. Not only is he expected to be gorgeous, rich, charming, dedicated and loyal, but he also has to be attracted to the most humble and meekest woman in town. The woman seems to sit back and wait to be chosen. Then after a kiss from her prince, she changes into a beautiful princess. He has everything and then he generously gives everything to her, the one with nothing. *Could it be that the fairy tale role we have created for men is so outlandish and unrealistic that we have actually set them up for failure?*

The expectations that women have make it almost impossible to be satisfied with any normal man without doing some very serious relationship adjustments. Then as life together progresses because of life experiences and realism women must learn to accept and be fairly happy with a partial prince. If he is not good looking, most women definitely want him to be financially successful and if he is not wealthy, most women want him to be gorgeous. In real life, so many men cannot and will never be those things; but yet they are good, loyal men and dedicated fathers. Although it has not been largely talked about or discussed, the prince image has made an unconsciously deep impact on men. *This expectation begins for them when the hope for a prince begins in women.* Although this marital image of marrying perfection has drastically decreased from what it was thirty, forty and fifty years ago, there is still an unspoken silence of expectation from the woman that contributes to her being unsatisfied after she gets married.

It is common and acceptable for women to want to "marry up." But it is a "new thing" for men to be comfortable with the idea of "marrying up." It is no longer something of which men are ashamed. Men are changing with the times and they feel that if the only way to become a prince is through marrying a "princess," then so be it. Many men feel that if successful and beautiful women want to marry them, then why should they refuse the offer?

Women too often have the Cinderella mentality and expect their partners to be willing to complete them. *When it becomes real to women that their men have problems and flaws then they seem worse than what they would have if women did not have unrealistic expectations in the first place.* Why would he want to marry you? Why is it his responsibility to rescue and save another person? It is an especially popular topic on the talk show circuit: women who make $25,000 annually but are arrogantly open to only dating men making six figures. While there are many stories where wealthy men want to marry women who are not as successful as they are and would actually prefer women whom they don't have to compete with financially, this often happens because they are looking for some other type of payoff. Men like this may feel *if you marry me for my money then I will marry you for your looks* and be looking for a trophy wife or a gorgeous bombshell. Many attractive women are okay with the idea that there is a tradeoff and with the fact that men are in love with their physical appearances; the downfall is that looks disappear and change over time. His money may never diminish and it also may actually increase, but looks fade away. If looks are the sole reason for a relationship it is likely that the man will start looking for a younger mate as his current partner ages. Unlike Cinderella, there is usually some cost and some benefit that the man is seeking if he is interested in a woman. Unless he is angelic and god-like, he is not seeking the lowest, meekest person whom he can come and rescue. A woman is going to have to supply for him something that he can't naturally get for himself.

As a society we need to create a whole different type of modern day fairy tale with the message: Prince Charming doesn't exist and Cinderella doesn't either. If we could get this message out without taking away the romanticism of love, hope and togetherness we might find that the role expectations for both genders are more realistic and therefore may help with our overall satisfaction in our future relationships.

As we mature and learn from our experiences and the experiences of other people, it is important that we create our own definition of a prince. *A prince is different things to different people.* Creating your own definition can be one key for relationship happiness and overall satisfaction. I feel the role of the prince is definitely changing and the definition is getting broader. What used to be the standard is no longer expected. Although there is and will always be an unspoken hope, our beliefs are slowly altering as we see and experience relationship failures and the overwhelming sense of unbalance many partners feel.

For many women, instead of having rich men in their lives their hopes have transferred to having hardworking men fill that role. For other women, the image of a gorgeous hunk can be replaced by someone who exercises and leads a healthy lifestyle. *Charming* is a word that you hardly ever hear anymore. Many women would agree that they would forget about the "charm" if he could just carry a good conversation consistently and if he would just open up and talk in a conversation on a regular basis. This could easily be defined as the new "charm."

I think that unconsciously women have somewhat come to terms with this redefinition, but they have not really settled it deep within their hopes and dreams. They have redefined their ideal men but at the same time they have not completely let go of their childhood hopes. They need desperately to settle the new ideals deep within their psyches so their relationships have better chances of achieving satisfaction. It is time that women tell themselves *a hardworking man who is trying to support his family every day turns me on.* It is also therapeutic to confess *although he may be losing his hair, his dimples will never go away.* Redefining what a prince is to you without the influence of Snow White or Cinderella might help save your marriage.

Although some women have successfully redefined their ideals of Prince Charming, the problem is that they have neglected to let the men in their lives know that their expectations have changed. Women want the best that they can find and they don't want to lessen their partners' motivation to "be all that they can be," *but if the image of Prince Charming has changed shouldn't they tell the prince?* The conflict of not acknowledging this change and not telling the change to the men in their lives can cause unwanted hurt, pain and dissatisfaction. It means that although women claim to be so modern and updated to the standards of today, one of the biggest parts of their worlds, which is relationships, is still old-fashioned and following the belief system of fairy tales. It has not changed and updated with the rest of women's lives.

Now, change has taken place in the action of what women do, like women working jobs that, many times, yield more money than men. But it is the unspoken chaos that has not done much changing. Women's belief and subtle expectations that they hold onto and the fact that they have not redefined the new prince is an example of the unspoken chaos. Isn't it ironic? The role of the woman has been loudly and publically changed, altered and redefined but there is still resistance and dissatisfaction with a man who does not follow the old standards of what a man should be. Today some old standards are somewhat looked down upon, such as the fight for respect when some women decide to be stay-at-home moms.

It is a confidence destroyer when a person doesn't believe she is good enough for her mate. It gets especially hurtful and abusive when the other mate also believes that his partner is not good enough and that he has, in fact, settled. I have come to believe the work and insecurity that happens when a person feels that his or her partner is someone way out of his or her league is simply not worth it. The entire relationship is filled with trying to be enough in every way to please your mate, yourself and everyone else. It is not uncommon that when a woman feels inadequate to her mate that she tries to make up the inadequacy in other areas. Women may become overly obsessed with their looks and begin to have feelings of unworthiness and insecurity along with worry and stress from trying to say and do everything perfect and correct all the time. The insecurity of feeling like he has his eyes on a more attractive or suitable woman can create jealousy that may be or may not be justified. *The truth is you really don't want to be married to Prince Charming anyways.*

10

Is There Any Hope?

As discussed previously, what a child sees has much more impact versus what he or she is told. When a child sees his or her parents acting in a way that eventually adds to the harmony in the child's life, he or she will almost always pick up some, if not all, of the habits. Can you image the impact and the surge of quality men if 60 or 80 percent of fathers were committed to showing respect to their wives? The influence on the overall male population would be amazing. The women would be happier, which in turn creates happier households, the men would be appreciated, loved and would have reestablished places of importance in the family and as parents and they would be able to physically show their children how to have successful families in the future.

Although this is a great idea for how to reestablish families, when there is clearly not an active father figure in the home it is hard to teach respect. *When the mother is the one who should be receiving respect it is hard for her to turn around and teach respect.* Unless it was taught and practiced in the home with her parents, she may really not understand the importance and the balance that it could bring. When the father is absent, all of the responsibility completely lies on the mother. She has to work, support, discipline, teach and love her family. These are arduous tasks. For her to have the time and the energy to teach her son the basics of finance, how to be courteous to women or how properly to do laundry, can seem impossible to an already overwhelmed mother.

We have already discussed how many boys are loved and not taught and that is the reason why they grow up to be loved men instead of taught men. This is not the sole reason for women outgrowing the men in their lives, but it is a major contributor to the problem. Again, all of this would be easier and more realistic if the father took his proper role as the legitimate teacher of his son and taught him things beyond mowing the lawn or working on cars. Although these skills are no doubt valuable, there are other basic skills, like paying the bills, helping around the house and being dedicated to a job, that also will help in his son's future. Because many men feel that they are criticized and nagged by their wives, it is important that wives allow fathers to teach their children in their own ways and in their own styles, without judgment or unasked opinion. Wives need to give genuine love and support. If more men knew that this was their responsibility and that they should become "givers" with their sons, we would see a new revolution in this area. More importantly, if the husband truly knew that he could take control of this aspect without being criticized, he would do so.

Women need to stop concluding that boys mature slower and need more time than the girls. Although this might be true in some cases, it is not true in all of them. Parents need to become much more objective and wait and see what their sons show about their personalities before parents assume. If it is clear after some time of observation that a son needs more time to catch up, mature and comprehend things, parents need to respect that. *Parents do this not by loving deeper but by teaching slower.* Remember, teaching is also a form of love.

Teaching a child does not mean excluding love from him or her; some experts argue that *teaching is actually a deeper level of love.* Teaching means that a parent has hope and confidence that his or her direction will increase the quality of children's lives. A teaching form of love involves faith, confidence and aspirations for a child that he or she will actually learn and absorb the things that are shared.

I feel there is lack of seminars, support teams and overall resources available for men today. It is hard to find a male social club. There was a time when almost every self-improvement program was geared toward the ability and growth of men, but things have quickly changed. There are many reasons for this change. Some people argue that there is a lack of programs and special events for men because men are not interested in such events. Recently I brought up this idea to a few men who were in my seminar and they mentioned, "Men don't usually even ask for directions so why would they be open to receiving help about their lives?" I think there is a lot of truth to that. In some ways too many men don't feel like they can learn anything from anyone, especially if it is not another man. Because there has been such a lack of programs and teachable moments historically for women, it breeds a whole different type of desire to learn and grow for them. There have been reports where experts have tried to organize male-based functions and women have become resentful that they were also not invited. We need a resurgence of programs to increase the confidence, responsibility and the role of men.

Although it is of a Jewish tradition, the celebration of the Bar Mitzvah has great purpose and does a wonderful job at placing responsibility and accountability on young men. According to Jewish law, when Jewish children reach the age of majority they become responsible for their actions and they become a Bar Mitzvah (Bat Mitzvah for girls). In many Conservative and Reform synagogues, children celebrate Bar and Bat Mitzvahs at age thirteen, which also coincides with physical puberty. Prior to this, the children's parents hold the responsibility for the children's adherence to Jewish law and tradition and, after this age, children bear their own responsibilities for Jewish ritual law, tradition and ethics and are privileged to participate in all areas of Jewish community life. Having a tradition and a standard way to recognize and celebrate a graduation to maturity is a tradition that all cultures need.

Most men are basically lone rangers. Too many of them don't have fathers who have actually taught them; there is not a support group to teach them how to properly be men and the few friends they have are no help because they are trying to figure out this relationship mystery themselves. Unfortunately men don't only have a lack of outside resources available to them but also many men lack strong and consistent male friendships. This might not be as true before marriage but too often after getting married men lose male companionships and lack valuable friendships. Because of the strength and the "giver" mentality of the woman, men tend to be around their wives the most. *What the wife does, the man will often do too.* Many times, their new friends become the friends that their wives know, not relationships that they have created on their own.

Most mothers lose their sons to their sons' wives. The wife has the power. She determines whom they are going to visit on the holidays. She actually establishes the tone for the entire family. In too many cases the husband just expects his wife to call the shots and he is happy to follow. Because men tend to stay into the whirlwind of allowing their wives to have most of the control they never get the help, direction and overall teaching they need.

The problem is that often the wife tries to teach her husband, but it is not her responsibility. Her level of teaching oftentimes is more about what she wants him to be for her, not what he needs to be in order to become a more whole and complete man. When she puts the energy into teaching him and he does not respond the way that she expects him to, *her teaching becomes a demand and her demand breeds relationship resentment.*

Many women want to marry men who are already complete and whole. They are not interested in trying to lead, educate and teach a man who is already supposed to be grown. They feel that amount of nurturing and energy should be focused on their children not their husbands and this is understandable. When it is clear that their relationship needs this type of one-on-one coaching and teaching it is hard to regain the same amount of respect and admiration that the wife once had for the husband. Once he starts learning and practicing what he has learned and it is obvious that he has grown, she looks at her more polished and manly husband with admiration. Depending on her previous resentment, she can't help but be reminded that she is actually the reason for his refinement, not him. That it was her patience, belief and knowledge that led him to be a better person and a more valuable man.

This new and improved man can unlock many different emotions to develop in his wife. When a woman finally sees improvements in this area, doubt, fear and worry can come. Of course, she is happy and relieved that he is better, more attentive and definitely more of the person she needs him to be, but she did not realize until now that when he was unpolished he was also less desirable to other women and definitely less of a threat. Before his transformation his confidence was low and he was not feeling as good about himself as he should have been. Regardless if she realized it or not, his lack of self-esteem increased her personal power. Although she knew that this was a problem, it also unconsciously was a comfort because he was less likely to stray and be desirable to other women.

This is not what women want and they become resentful at the thought, but we will see later in this chapter that changing your mindset in this area might be the key to salvaging your relationship.

Right Now Solutions

There is, of course, no way to go back and teach husbands' mothers how to teach and instruct their sons and then teach the fathers how to be role models of respect for both their sons and their daughters. We need "right now" solutions for "right-now" problems. However, when we truly understand that this issue is both complex and historical it is easier to have more understanding and decrease the blame toward husbands.

When women internalize that men are just basically acting out what they have been taught, it allows women to have more love and less resentment toward them.

When it is clear that a man is worth keeping and both partners are willing to work on improving the relationship, then this relationship definitely would be worth investing time and energy into. It is important that partners are clear about this or energy is either going to go to a useful place or a place that will just breed more resentment and strife. It is totally up to the couple where they put it.

When women are fighting internally with their mates, men oftentimes don't even know that a fight is going on. It is common that when a woman reaches this level of outgrowth of her relationship, she is in a constant level of resentment and anger.

She is simply angry at him "all the time", regardless if she acts out or not.

Many times men are caught off-guard because on one day she *seems* okay. But they neglect to understand that if the argument from two days ago has not been truly resolved and if there is not a verbal commitment to do better, women are more than likely still brewing over it. Women's frustration and hurt just piles and piles on top; it does not go away like men often seem to think. Men often make the grave mistake of simply accepting what they see and seeing what they see only. With women it is usually much deeper and complex.

For men, more often than not, it is not in what they see in their women, it is in what women already said to their men that counts. It is best to assume that even when things seem normal a woman is still angry.

Unless the problem has been resolved, a woman may be still focused on that anger and problems even though time has passed. She might be willing to still have sex with her partner, but it is more about her getting fulfilled not the man. Every day it becomes clearer to her that things will probably never change unless something drastic happens. So oftentimes the fight becomes more internal than external. The woman gets tired of fuming and getting ignored. She runs out of ideas on how to clearly relay that she needs more consideration and help from her mate. Because the nagging does not seem to work, she finds herself holding in her emotions.

Holding in emotions breeds more anger and it brews resentment. She becomes her personality: tired, frustrated and disappointed with her life. The fight becomes inside. Sometimes she is tired and other times she is angry but there is an internal fight that she is not able to stop. This internal fight becomes very dangerous for the husband and often it surprises him. Given the case that men will usually base their present realities on what they see, they believe that if their wives are not nagging or arguing that they must be okay and everything is fine. She is acting okay so she must be okay. They have no idea that their wives have taken this outgrowth and imbalance issue to a whole different level. For him, it is the fact that he does not pick up his underwear: That is the depth of it. For her, it is a matter of respect, love and overall commitment.

Men are often shocked when wives reach the point where they are asking for divorces. A man is usually shocked and unprepared for such a strong accusation and conclusion because he did not pick up his underwear. Not picking up the underwear is all he sees. That is the part of the nagging that he actually gets. Deep down he realizes that he should pick up his underwear. However, by the time he gets around to doing it, she has already picked it up for him, so he will often ask himself *What it the use anyway?* The woman, on the other hand, sees this "picking up the underwear" as a small segment of a much bigger issue. For her, it is not about picking up the underwear; this is simply the example she used to describe to him what she needed. His mistake is that he took what she said literally word for word. For her, it is more about overall respect and consideration. *It is not only about picking up the underwear, not initiating dates or not giving her intimate attention unless he wants sex; it is not one thing in particular. It is about him treating her like she is his mother instead of his wife.* It is about him seeing himself as a partner who shares in making the household run smoothly. It is the partnership that he willingly gives just because he does not want her to be overloaded and overwhelmed.

I believe the men who have it figured out need to teach the men who haven't. Most men would listen to the direction and words of other men whom they respect and admire. I think it has to be a male figure whom they see as knowledgeable and successful in his own relationship. Too many men find it hard to listen to the voice and direction of a female if it is not their own mothers. Now, there are always exceptions and there are some men who see their wives as their best friends. When this is the case, the resentment of outgrowth does not usually get to a level that threatens the relationship.

If some of the more seasoned husbands and fathers who had to figure out for themselves the mystery of pleasing their wives would teach or communicate with those who still do not know, it would do wonders. For the untaught to realize that there is hope and a solid strategy to solving this problem, it would be amazing and revolutionary. Knowing how to maintain harmony, increase the love and be appreciated while still keeping their manhood is knowledge most men would appreciate.

The problem is that too many seasoned husbands still don't know themselves. Yes, maybe the nagging has decreased and maybe the tension has seemed to simmer down, but their once carefree and fun-loving wives have either grown independent or bitter because their relationship problems have never really been resolved.

Some men who have actually figured it out neglect to communicate and share the secrets with their sons, friends and family members, because they have no idea how big of a problem this really is. They don't realize that secrets they have learned can help keep the structure of the family from deteriorating. Many don't see that the confidence of men is being destroyed every day, because they have lost purpose and meaning in their families and with their children.

It is more like the female personality to share and exchange information. Women tell other women secrets about how to live better and more abundantly all the time. It is not uncommon for women to get pearls of wisdom from women in just passing and innocent conversation. It is usually not in the nature of men to seek advice from others and try to find a better way.

11

For Men Only:
How to Play the Game

When a Man Feels He's Been Outgrown

It is hard for most men to admit or to get "real" with their feelings enough to admit that they feel that they have been outgrown by their wives. A man may feel that something in his relationship takes away from his ego and leaves him with a sense of emptiness, but labeling and admitting his wife no longer feels he's adequate is difficult and disheartening. Most men link what they are feeling to an emotion that makes them feel left behind or not included, as though their existences and everyday presences have lost value and meaning in their households. Many of the men in this situation would say that they feel they are more of a problem in their families than a help. Many experts agree that unless this relationship problem is rectified and solved quickly the feeling of being "left behind" swells into resentment, embarrassment and confusion. It swells because this feeling of being left behind is always complimented by a wife who is also unhappy, unsatisfied and angry.

By the time the problem gets to a level of embarrassment, there have been escalating arguments and hurtful words exchanged between the two partners that can't be taken away. He no longer feels that he can satisfy his wife on any level. Because of the possibility of causing another argument and increasing the anger, he is afraid of trying anything new to make things better. *Communication, sex and spending time together quickly become less important and he finds himself spending more time away from home just to avoid the conflict. He does not realize that the more time he spends away from home the more upset and angry his wife becomes.* For her the answer to the problem is for the husband to be at home and make a difference, not trying to escape from home so that he can ignore the fact that a problem exists.

Here are some secrets for men and some new revelations for modern day women.

Foreplay Begins in the Kitchen

Sex is very different for women than it is for men. Unfortunately, it seems to change for some women after they get married. Before marriage there are no prerequisites. Sex just happens and oftentimes it is initiated by her. Then when life starts getting overwhelming, after the marriage, there are a million other things for the wife to do and sexual relations suffer. Women become frustrated when their husbands do not understand the sudden change in priorities or why some women see sex as a chore instead of an act in which partners get closer. Often women do not verbalize the pressures and changes they feel so their partners do not understand why they do not get passionate intimacy as the marriage progresses. Sex seemed so easy and natural before and then when they carry this same standard of "expecting something for nothing" into the marriage women start feeling that they are getting used and taken for granted. Again, men have simply mastered and then put into practice what women have so successfully taught them.

When trying to restore a relationship it is only fair that women get truly honest and transparent with their mates and tell them, "I realize that before marriage I taught you that sex comes with simply asking, but since life is steadily becoming more complex and stressful, it takes more now to get me in the mood." Women need to make their partners aware that sharing the chores and pressures of family and home life together, even little things like helping with the dishes without being asked and stopping the kids from playing favorites, turns women on. Men's love and sensitivity make women more passionate toward their husbands when in bed. *When a woman consistently praises and encourages her mate when he does something right then she is actually re-teaching him how to treat her.*

Men truly don't understand that it becomes a "sex" thing when they help around the house and when women can depend and lean on them, regardless of the circumstances. The appreciation factor often is demonstrated by how open, available and responsive women are in the bedroom. If a woman resents the fact that her husband repeatedly did not take out the trash leaving it for her to do, she doesn't feel in the mood for sex. *If the husband can make her life better outside of the bedroom, she will respond completely inside of the bedroom.*

Don't Listen to What She Says

Whatever wives say, their husbands shouldn't listen. When a man actually listens to his wife, he will often take what she has said literally. But one of the worst mistakes a man can make is actually listening to his wife. Men have to start reading between the lines. It is always bigger, much bigger, than what a woman is actually saying. If she says, "You never tell me I look pretty anymore", what she is really saying is, "Are you still attracted to me?" When she says, "There is too much pressure on me", what she is really saying is, "Please help me. I don't feel appreciated." Men need to also understand that statements are often questions and questions are often statements. *It is bigger than what the man hears and it is so much bigger than what the woman has actually said.*

Do Something Different to Get Something Different

The first thing that a man needs to do is to simply *want to see things differently* in his relationship with his wife. I know most men don't want to be nagged or unappreciated by their wives but many don't spend the time and effort to reflect on what their wives really need. Now, in order to try and make a change, *men need to believe that things can change.* It should be clear that if a man keeps doing what he has always done, he will keep getting what he has been getting. *If a man thinks the way that he has always thought then he will get what he has always gotten.*

One of the major problems with men in this area is that they don't really believe that things can be different. They really believe that all relationships result in being nagged by women. They might have been conditioned to believe this by watching their mothers and how they became disgusted with their husbands or by seeing sisters nag their brothers-in-law. This tendency to nag and communicate frustration can also be done by the mother to the son. The son is just a smaller example and extension of the husband. Too many men believe that men can't do anything right and that all women yell and fuss over small things.

When a man begins a relationship believing it will be a certain way and when what he thought was going to happen starts happening, he feels that it is just his "turn." Many men truly feel that women can't be satisfied. That there is no way they can be happy. When this is what the man believes, it is easier for men to separate themselves from the problems and the blame.

Men believe that it really is not about them; it is just about women's intense personalities. Many different situations confirm his belief, such as when she becomes easily upset with their son's teacher over the fact that he was held inside for recess or when she confronts the contractor who did not follow through on what he or she promised. The husband just sees his wife as stressed out and bitter. He neglects to understand that she is more sensitive and more willing to confront others because her entire life has become a fight and a battle. Unfortunately, being unhappy is becoming part of her norm. She is tired of people not following through inside her home and outside her home.

Men Need to Become More Like Women

Regardless of which way one looks at it and which way one sums up the conclusion, the woman's liberation movement has caused women to be more like men! To better explain this, there are books that have reached the best seller list that teach women "how to be effective leaders and still keep their femininity." There are also books about why men are seen as assertive but when women use the same skill they are seen as a "bitches." More and more books teach women how to *act like a woman but think like a man*.

Yes, the movements have bred more confident, assertive and take charge women. Assertiveness has for too long been seen as masculine. Some women have become experts on how to be feminine when they *need* to be and assertive when they *have* to be. They have blended their personalities and have learned to be both feminine and masculine.

Unfortunately, many men have lost some of their natural qualities of speaking up and being assertive. Too often when they practice these skills they are seen as being aggressive, dangerous and unsafe. For them to hold on to who they naturally are can sometimes be a disadvantage because there are so many men who have denied or neglected to practice this side of their natural selves.

I feel men could profit by learning the secrets of becoming more feminine while still holding onto their manhood. When they can successfully learn this they will master how to play the game. *This skill and willingness can give them great success in every aspect of their lives. It is called connectedness in the business world. It is charisma in intimate relationships and it is described as empathy in relationships with children.* The key for men is to create balance in their personalities and still be seen as men.

Is it feminine to communicate directly and honestly even when it does create a disagreement? Is it feminine to really listen to both the words and the emotion behind what a partner is saying or is it simply respectful? Initiating date night and hand-holding without expecting sex in return could be expressing that a man appreciates and sees his wife as a real person who needs affection. Many times men get in such a rut with who they have become. Given all the negative things they see in the media about males they have learned to believe and these things make them neglect to see how simple it is to work on connecting to the one to whom they were once attracted. *The same work and effort that the man put into the relationship to secure his wife should increase twofold to keep her after the marriage.*

Although this is rarely talked about, most men would agree that what they are actually attracted to a woman who has a balance of both feminine and masculine qualities—a woman who is feminine enough to wear a dress sometimes and comfortable positioning herself as the receiver in the relationship but who is also masculine enough to be independent and confident in challenging situations instead of needy. This ability to balance gender traits goes beyond what is needed in both personal and professional lives. It is actually the key to being a "turn-on" to the opposite sex. Balance is an attractive quality both men and women look for in a mate. Many women think they want mysterious, quiet, strong men, but I feel that though this may be what attracts a woman initially to her mate, once she starts increasing her involvement with him she desires for him to be more open, honest and empathetic.

You Already Have Everything She Needs

After all the male bashing, nagging and negative portrayals of men the media has created, it is understandable why men need to be reminded and encouraged that they can be both sensitive and strong. The lack of resources, programs and strong male models confirms even more that they need encouragement in this area. Sometimes men feel that their mates are asking them to be something and to become someone they don't know how to be. If a man understood that everything his partner needs him to be is already inside him, it would automatically raise his confidence.

Now it may be buried, perhaps it is covered or maybe he does not now know how to get to it, but without a doubt a man already has everything that he needs to be, both for himself and for his mate. The ability to communicate and open up is already there. He might be used to not talking or trusting others with his feelings, but the ability to talk more and share his feelings is already in him. He cannot do it exactly like a woman but he can do it like a man perfectly. He can also do things such as picking up his underwear off the floor and helping with the laundry. Most men, just like women, have an innate need for order and structure. A man might have become used to chaos and mess but deep down he feels the need to lessen the chaos and increase order as strongly as a woman does. Because he loves his children, he also realizes the importance of being part of their everyday lives, teaching them to do their homework and to straighten up their rooms. Children need their fathers to help them master small as well as large tasks.

If a man knew that a woman can never teach a growing son how to be a "real" man, that only a man can teach a boy this essential rite of passage, it would give him more purpose and meaning in the house. Similarly, he needs to understand that his daughter will listen to him much more intensely about choosing the right boyfriend, because he has had firsthand experience on how a man thinks. In relationships and families, there are things that women are equipped to do and there are things that men are more emotionally prepared to do; despite the abuse, the labels and even their own personal beliefs, men's ability to give in the way that they have been designed to do will never go away.

Make Love to Her with Her Clothes On

I believe the way to a woman's heart is to make love to her with her clothes on. When a woman feels she has been touched, caressed and held just because she is wanted and desired without sex being the conclusion, a man has found the key to her heart. After ten years of marriage, when a husband still will kiss his wife longer than ten seconds or when he reaches out to hold her hand when walking together, it will erase a lot of mistakes.

Last summer, Gail, one of my new clients, stressed how unhappy she was in her marriage. She was considering separating from her husband. She confided to me that her husband rarely touched her outside of the bedroom. She said she did not realize anything was wrong until she started noticing how her daughter's husband was consistently affectionate to her daughter, even after seven years of marriage. She mentioned that her son-in-law's hands were always affectionately on his wife "just because." Gail did not expect anything from her husband until she saw the affection that her daughter was getting from her own husband. My client was hurt, disappointed and jealous that she was not getting the same attention.

I told her that her husband had responded to the rules that she initially laid out for him in their marriage. As she came to understand this, she started remembering how at the beginning of the marriage he too was affectionate, just like her daughter's husband, but she shrugged him off. Having taught him that she was not open to affection, Gail's husband did not offer it. Gail saw that the communication she gave her husband in the beginning of their marriage was the reason for her current unhappiness.

I told Gail in order to re-teach her husband, she needed first to be honest. Gail had to apologize for shrugging off his hand and denying his kiss and explain to him it was not until recently that she realized the importance of affection. I mentioned to her that for a while she might need to be the one who initiates "lovemaking with the clothes on." After a while, when her husband discovers that this is a *real request and not just a feeling that will be gone tomorrow,* she will successfully reignite the affection that he once had within him.

Still be Her Boyfriend

Just like women are guilty of looking casual, wearing sweatpants and stopping sex, men also change after marriage. Most women don't know how to actually put it into words, but what they really want from their husbands is for them to continue to be their boyfriends. The same effort that a man gives to the relationship before the marriage is the same energy that the woman wants after the marriage. Whatever a man does to impress and connect to a woman before the wedding is what she's expecting after the union.

While both parties are guilty of not fulfilling expectations of their marriage, I believe if one partner held to his or her responsibility, it would cause the other to respond as well. If a wife wears the same heels and makeup that got her husband's attention before the wedding, he might be more motivated to take her out on the town on regular date nights. If he continues to make his wife a priority over his friends, she might be prompted to do more of the activities he likes with him. One reaction triggers the next.

See Yourself as Her

It would change each partner's perspective and viewpoint completely if he or she could see him or herself as the other person for one day. If the woman could imagine and be really honest with herself about how she would feel if she had to live with herself, she might finally understand her mate's point. She should ask herself: *Am I overly critical? Is it impossible to please me? Am I in bad moods more than good ones? Do I nag?* If the woman answered these questions without trying to justify the reasons causing her actions, words and feelings, it would help her understand her partner's criticisms and reasoning. This same insight goes also for men. If for one day a man could imagine himself from his partner's vantage point, he should ask himself: *Am I inconsiderate and lazy? Do I share the tasks for the household? Could I do more? Am I silent or angry a lot of the time? Do I understand why she is unhappy and feels unappreciated? Could I do more to make her feel loved, appreciated and beautiful?*

As human beings we get so caught up in ourselves that we very rarely look beyond our own feelings and try to understand what our partners feel or what they are going through. If the truth were to be explored, in most cases women would understand why men are turned off by their behavior and men would understand that their wives have way too much responsibility for the home and family. When partners reach that understanding, one of the most important steps to take after is to let the other person know that he or she finally understands why the partner feels a certain way. This would open up a flow of connectedness and communication for the future.

One Plus One Should Not Equal One

It is a shame that in a marriage so many husbands still need to be reminded that one plus one should equal two. Other than the possible ongoing access to sex, it is easy to still feel lonely and alone while being married. It is not uncommon for two people to get married and live more as strangers after the marriage than they did before. This is because there is a tendency to stop trying to please and connect to a partner.

When they began their relationship, my friend Barbara was forty-eight and her boyfriend Fred was fifty-four. Barbara had no children, but Fred had several and all of them were grown. It was a shock when I found out that they were getting married, because although I considered myself good friends with Barbara, I was not aware that she was seeing anyone seriously. This would be Fred's third marriage and Barbara's first. When we met Fred, whom Barbara had described as wealthy, attractive and intelligent, I must admit that both my husband and I were disappointed. Barbara has always been beautiful, soft-spoken, smart and focused on her professional career. Fred seemed like he was more street smart, casual and not really attentive to Barbara's needs. Fred had the tendency to mumble when he talked and he often seemed distracted and unfocused. Barbara had a successful career, a beautiful home and had made sound and smart financial decisions in her life. Though well-off financially, Fred lived with his mother, whom he said he helped out. He had investments but did not work steadily. They moved away after the marriage.

A few years later when they visited, Barbara told me that she was definitely disappointed in her marriage and if she could do it all over again she would not have married Fred. I asked Barbara about the other attributes Fred brought to the marriage beyond his wealth. When one gains a companion or a spouse, I believe it must mean more than what he or she can offer financially. Barbara revealed Fred's companionship was lacking, that he was not home most evenings and she was not sure where he spent a great deal of his time. When they were home together, she was usually in the bedroom and he was in the family room. They had limited conversation. Although they talked about going on vacation together or having consistent date nights twice a month, these things never actually happened. Barbara mentioned that her life really was as lonely as before she got married, despite the fact that she had a partner for sex and another person living in the house.

One plus one should not equal one. Women of today are becoming more expansive in their thinking about good partners for marriage. Many successful women are saying, "I really don't need his money, but it would be nice to have a companion to do things with or just someone whom I can respect and share my life with." Things are definitely changing and the roles and needs of both men and women are transforming. Some of these areas are finances, companionship, friendship and duties and responsibilities at home. When one adds a companion or spouse, other changes in both partners' lives should follow. Too often men still want to live separately and independently after they are married. Marriage needs to be a partnership of mind, spirit and body. Otherwise the union does not make sense.

Let Go of the Need to be Right

Many times the reason for conflict and anger is not about the dispute or the principles behind the dispute; it is simply the need to be right. It is more about ego than anything. It is not uncommon for couples to be in long-term arguments or disputes and after some time has passed they don't even remember why they are arguing. Often they don't understand that the reason behind most disputes is the need to be right.

When a person brings this type of mentality into a marriage it is hard to overcome. One of the most powerful things a man can do is not battle with having to be right all the time. Not only is it impossible but it is also unrealistic and shallow. Many experts agree that when people battle with letting go of their egos in this way, it is usually a sign of low self-esteem. It is a sign that they have the need to hide behind the persona of being perfect instead of showing their true selves.

When my son was young, I was a little put off when my husband so easily apologized and showed a vulnerable side in their relationship. It was a "turnoff" for me at first, because I simply thought he was too quick to say that he was sorry when he really did not do anything wrong. But as my son grew older, my husband's willingness to be transparent and to admit that he did not always know best created a special bond between them. I really became aware that my husband was a dedicated, caring and very committed father. His behavior also modeled for my son that a strong man is one who doesn't have the need to be right all the time.

Who She Was Before the Marriage

Men will often expect their girlfriends to continue to have the same personalities, mentalities and care-free dispositions when they become their wives. However, both the man and woman should in some ways transform into the people that they need to be in order to take care of their marital responsibilities.

Life after marriage requires a personality change. The more stress and responsibility in a woman's life the more changes occur. This is usually a result of being overwhelmed and stressed, sometimes because of having children. A woman before the responsibilities of marriage and children is an entirely different person afterwards. Additionally, the responsibility of taking care of business and the household requires more changes. Who a partner is before the marriage is not who he or she is going to be after the marriage. *Often, how much she changes after the marriage depends on how much support her husband gives her in the marriage.* She is more likely to remain fun-loving, like she was pre-marriage, if she feels appreciated in the home.

Men often wonder what happened to the women with whom they fell in love and they neglect to see that the attributes are still there but buried underneath the seriousness of life. The more the husband can share the seriousness and the responsibilities with her, the more the traits and personality he fell in love with before the marriage will survive.

You Can't Do Everything

Because we are human beings, we will never be good at everything. Many times a partner is just looking for willingness from his or her mate to understand and do more. A woman needs to feel that she is being heard and a husband's listening means to her that he is respecting her. If a man can relay to his wife that he understands and that he is willing to do whatever it takes to make things better, he will become a happy man because he will have a happier wife.

Some men are not good at helping the kids with their homework or at doing the laundry. What men need to do is look deep within themselves and discover what is it that they are good at. No one is expecting his or her partner to be good at everything. A man does not have to commit to doing everything and doesn't have to pretend that he can do things at the speed and the thoroughness of his wife, but he shows his support by being willing to do more without being asked.

Men need to tell their wives how they will contribute and what they can realistically do each day and each week to help even the load. This will begin to touch wives' hearts. Once men commit to tasks, they must be sure they follow through and don't slack. *Remember, it is not so much what a man does, but that he shows his wife that he is willing to share the burdens, duties and responsibilities of the household.*

How to Know When There is Trouble

It is about mind over matter: If you don't mind, then it will not matter. My husband has always said that a man can always tell when there is something wrong with his spouse. There are two things can happen. Either she becomes very quiet and distant or she becomes very verbal about her complaint. It depends on the personality of the woman how she will express her concern.

Most men say that they would prefer a woman to be quiet and not yell and scream when she is upset. Although I very much understand the reasoning behind this, I feel when a woman is quiet it is much more onerous than when she is verbal. With a verbal woman it is more obvious that she is upset. A man is not caught by surprise, because she has very verbally expressed that she is unhappy. When a woman is verbal about her complaint it also conveys that she still has deep feelings and is willing to fight for the relationship. If she did not care she would not be so verbal.

When a women elects to keep her feelings inside then it is harder to determine what she is thinking and what the ramifications may be. Discomfort and uncertainty start brewing. She actually holds the power and the control when she keeps her partner wondering. When I say that she has more power in her silence, I am not talking about when she is quiet with an attitude or when she is quiet and pouting; these are not power but signs of immaturity. I am referring to a quietness that produces calmness, which often occurs when a woman gets to the point that she no longer cares and feels the situation is simply not worth an argument. This is when the marriage is in deep trouble. After this point she is often not turning back. *Those who love the least have the most power.*

Nagging is Good
Those who love hard also fight hard. This saying always proves itself to be true. A woman would not nag if she did not care and did not believe that there was hope still in the relationship. If she is nagging her husband he still has a chance to reconnect to her heart.

Romance is the Man's Responsibility
In this discussion of romance, I am referring to the affection and respect outside of the bedroom. This may be a shock to many men, but men have the responsibility of initiating and keeping the romance going in relationships. This whole notion and practice became distorted when women started positioning themselves as the givers. Women took on the complete responsibility to make everything happen in relationships. When women become everything, they take it upon themselves to establish the romantic tone and to schedule the dates. Then when they get married they become resentful for what they did to themselves.

When a husband notices that his wife is taking on the responsibility of romance, he does not feel a need to contribute anymore. The husband learns to bring flowers only on special occasions or when she is angry with him, because she is in charge. Although the woman tends to take charge in this area, she should not be expected to. It also can bruise a male's ego when the woman takes this responsibility away from him.

Power and Money

A man will never lose women chasing money but he will lose money chasing women. It is so important to stay focused on accomplishing goals, having a personal mission and simply learning to play the game. We hear stories over and over again about how politicians and attractive celebrities have been caught having multiple affairs when they have built their reputations on being decent and ethical family men.

Power and women are the two things that can satisfy a man's mind, body and soul. It is interesting that when a man has either power or women the other automatically comes. When a man acquires a certain amount of power, women tend to follow. Some women love men with authority, respect and power. It becomes a status statement for these women to be able to get this type of man. Men tend to have more access to women based on the power that he has acquired. It often is a gender weakness for men and the very thing that speaks to a man's self-worth and societal accomplishments. A focused man with a vision is one who can have both women and power. Men tend to lose money, reputation, status and self-respect by chasing women.

12

Are You Worth the Change
He Will Need to Make?

As we've concluded, you are not the same person you used to be. You are now a more mature and complex woman due to your life experiences. If you decide to stay in your relationship some realizations are necessary.

Regardless of the outgrowth and the reasons behind it, there is no way that the situation is entirely his fault. *Even if you are guilty of simply allowing his problems, behavior and actions toward you, you are partly to blame.* Can you be forgiven for secretly expecting him to read your mind? Have you distorted his image with family, friends and possibly your children by talking behind his back about what he is not doing and what his flaws are? *As well as asking can you forgive him, you need to ask can he forgive you.* Can he trust you with the rest of his life? Can he trust that you will handle him with care and love during the times when he knows and when he does not know better?

If the problem is not too far gone and the hurt is not at an all time high, look closely at what you should consider:

♦ **Understand your pluses in the work world can be problem areas in your marriage**. If you are assertive and bold at your job, you might have to work on being patient and less demanding in your home life. Being a natural leader may cause your partner to label you as critical and bossy.

♦ **Can your ego handle a new and improved man?** If your mate becomes renewed and improved, more sensitive and caring, you may begin to feel a little insecure and confused. You may ask yourself, *Does he still want me? Am I enough for him?* Although it is common for these questions to arise, it is unhealthy to want your mate to stay as he is so that you can feel more sure of yourself.

♦ **Your problem saying no just might be a big problem.** There is no secret that women from every walk of life and with all different types of educational backgrounds are taught from childhood to be pleasers. Women battle with speaking up and have the tendency to take on more tasks than they realistically can do. After women have said yes when they should have said no, too many of them have the tendency to blame others for their problems. In your relationship there might be obvious outgrowth, but is it possible that you are overwhelmed most of the time and have a problem saying no. You may be overwhelmed outside of your marriage, be it with parents, at work or even in your social life, simply because you always say yes.

♦ **I didn't believe we would be happy anyway.** We often can become so conditioned to see and hear the negative that we don't know how to actually see and expect the good. As a society we have been trained and taught to see and focus on what it not going right. *Your perspective is your reality*. You create your reality with your perspective. Some women who believe that they are strong oftentimes have low self-esteem, because they don't believe that they will ever really be happy anyway. Some women think their husbands are jerks because they predicted that they would be. Some people are scared of having successful relationships. For many women it can hurt less to be disappointed than to be open to love.

♦ **Pick three things you need to have.** I often tell my clients to find three things that they must have in their relationships and then see how their men measure up. We should expect about 80 percent of what we want and be willing to teach and be flexible with the other 20 percent; this is a realistic perspective.

♦ **He really does want to please you.** Most men really do want to be princes on white horses, the one on whom a woman can depend. But if relationship mishaps have caused him to believe that he does not have what it takes to please his wife, he will start losing hope. Many men see it as personal failures when they are not making the ones they love happy. The last thing they want to do is to feel like they are causing personal hardship in their mates' lives. So many times women forget that men do have personal needs and desires to feel that they are important and that they have added to another's life.

♦ **Don't apologize to other women just because you have something good.** After being married for some time, my husband passionately reminded me that I don't have to apologize to other women verbally or through my actions for having a good relationship with him. He said I shouldn't hide the diamond he gave me and I shouldn't downplay the closeness of our family. It was not until my husband said this that I realized I had been doing just what he accused me of: downplaying my healthy and loving relationship, because I did not want other women to feel bad or jealous. I learned from my husband that in no way should I flaunt or brag about the love we have, but it is not up to me to make everyone else feel better by minimizing my good fortune. You don't have to minimize your husband's love for you because so many other women have not found Mr. Right.

13

Self Reflections

Would You Want You?
Here are some questions to consider about your problems maintaining a fulfilling relationship:

♦ Would you want to have sexual relations with you?
♦ In public, would you be proud of you?
♦ Would you want to deal with your personality everyday?
♦ Would you want to marry, live with and spend a lifetime with you?

If you can honestly answers yes to at least three of these questions then you have several positive attributes. If not, perhaps you need to consider some serious work on yourself.

Thought: *It is so easy to be harsh and critical toward mates concerning how they treat us. We have all been guilty of looking at situations from a one-sided perspective, which is usually our own. When we truly consider the question "would you want to marry you?" it very graciously brings on a whole new outlook and perspective of what our mates are truly dealing with. It allows us to get real with the fact that most of us might not be interested in marrying ourselves.*

Ignore the Facts and Look at the Truth

When you are in a serious relationship with a person it is important not to allow facts to get in the way of your ascertaining the truth about him. There is a distinct difference between the two and most people go through their entire relationships without fully comprehending this. For example, your husband may have the tendency to talk too much and give too much detail; this is a *fact* about him. But although he talks a lot and is full of instructions, he is an awesome father; this is the *truth* about him.

Many times in our relationships, we make the grave mistake of giving the facts about a person the same respect and attention that we give the truth. From another perspective, your mate might be a reliable provider, which is a fact about him, but is also abusive, which is the truth. In a relationship the facts are not as important as the truth.

Thought: *Look at the truth behind your relationship.*

Necessary Boundaries and Rules

It is important to have some boundaries and rules that you are not willing to compromise and to get professional help if you find you are in a harmful relationship. Such limits may include:

♦ He is addicted to prescription or illegal drugs or sex.
♦ He gives attractive female strangers more attention than he gives you.
♦ He wants you to do things that make you uncomfortable, such as sexual acts, lying, cheating or stealing.

- He looks at pornography on a regular basis
- He tends to belittle women and it is obvious that he feels that they are less than and not as important as the male gender.
- He has severe mood swings and his behavior is unpredictable.

Is it Not about Communication

It is time to discount everything you have heard about communication, *because it is not about communication; it is about connection.* We can communicate all day long and talk and talk and have a one-sided conversation. To get to your husband's heart and enter the level of having a healthy friendship can never be accomplished by mere communication. It has to be done through forming a better connection. Here are questions that have proven to form a connection and have gone beyond the realm of mere communication:

- When are you the happiest?
- What is your greatest accomplishment so far?
- What do you want to accomplish in your life that you have not had the chance to do yet?
- Whom do you admire the most in your circle of friends and family and why?
- What do you like the most about yourself?
- What do you desire to change about yourself?

Answering these questions with your mate will move your relationship into a realm of trust, authenticity and true friendship.

Thought: *When you seek to understand your mate on this level you must also reveal these same answers about yourself so that your relationship reaches a new level of connection.*

The Most Dangerous Phrase

"All men are dogs" is a phrase that many are conditioned to believe. Women are aware that there are too many men who are not commitment material and are not safe people with whom to have a relationship. But to conclude that "all men are dogs" is unfair to the entire male population. When a woman makes such a conclusive statement, this also includes her sons, father, brothers and uncles. Every man she knows is included in this statement and they don't have a chance to be seen as decent because they are men. For outsiders to conclude that someone's son, brother or uncle is "no good" because he is male is unfair. After hearing and saying that "all men are dogs," it is common to become conditioned and desensitized to quality good men. This negative belief starts showing in how women talk to men, how they perceive men and what they expect from men. This is one of the most dangerous phrases to have in one's vocabulary. It would be the same unfairness for men to state that all women are "whores" just because they are women. For society to be so conclusive because of a few bad apples is not fair.

Thought: *Just remember, when the phrase "all men are dogs" casually crosses your mind, think about how annoyed you would be if other women concluded that your son or father was a "dog" just because he is male.*

Do Women Really Want Their Men to be Women?

Women often want men to talk and ramble on with unending energy just like women tend to do. They would love for men to be patient, interested and give shopping advice like other women. They would be in heaven if the men in their lives could think, talk and multitask just like their girlfriends. Is it fair to say that often women become more and more annoyed by their husbands because they don't act like women? *It is so hard for men to be what women want.* If a man acts like a man, he is judged to be distant and uncommunicative; if he acts softer and shows real feelings and emotions, women may then see him as weak and wimpy.

Thought: *Women must balance their need for sensitivity in their mates with their need for strength.*

Treat Yourself Well

It would be so unfair to expect others, especially men, to treat you better than what you treat yourself. To expect others to give you more respect, care and attention than you actually are willing to give yourself is too much to ask and expect. Just as we teach people how to treat us by what we will accept from them, *people usually give you the equivalent amount of respect that they see come from you and in you. This respect is usually based on your own actions.* For us to expect more from others than what we have been conditioned to do for ourselves is not reasonable.

Thought: *You teach people how much respect to give you by how much respect you give yourself.*

The Way to a Man's Heart is to Receive

We have explored the fact that too many women are non-stop superwomen who are constantly going and constantly doing for others both at home and at work. When you are so accustomed to doing everything yourself then it is hard to receive at the same time. It is difficult to both give and receive. Men, on the other hand, innately have the need to give.

In Eastern philosophy, the concept of feminine and masculine is called yin and yang. I learned to understand this concept through this illustration: Every tangible object consists of both yin (feminine) and yang (masculine). For a vase, the yang is the structure of the vase itself and the yin is the empty part in the center of the vase. The yin is the most important part of the vase because it holds the flowers. There would be no value in the vase if there were no flowers. The yin is the part that receives and the yin also gives the yang purpose.

I am not saying that the woman is the most important part of a relationship, but I am saying that the woman is supposed to be the "yes" person and she is the one who initially determines if the relationship is going to progress. From this standpoint she does play a very significant role.

Men must feel that they have a purpose for their mates and that there is a need for them. For example, when a man asks if his wife needs help with carrying the groceries and she replies, "No, I have it. I do this all the time", it takes away the purpose of the man. He knows when he offers to help that his wife is capable of handling the groceries for herself but he also knows that it might make her life just a little easier if he is allowed to help.

It is impossible to receive and control at the same time. Women need to learn how to receive without it feeling to them like they are giving up their femininity.

Thought: *Rejecting the gift is rejecting the giver.*

He is Interviewing, Not You

When talking with men many women make the common mistake of trying to fill in every space, every pause of silence, with words. When women do this they are working too hard. A good relationship is one where the conversation can naturally flow. When women take on the responsibility of trying to keep the conversation going, they again fall into the role of giver. The person takes on the responsibility of making sure everyone is comfortable and becomes the one who must think hard for the next word.

As mentioned previously, women have forgotten or never truly known that they are the receivers, not the givers. Before women actually get to know the personalities of their dates they start working harder to make sure that things keep going. From the very beginning women make the grave mistake of working hard instead of relaxing and having fun in the relationship. Women try to look sexy even when they are physically uncomfortable, they take on the responsibility of keeping the relationship moving forward, they take on the task to schedule every date and they take on the responsibility of making sure the excitement is strong. *Women have prematurely invested the energy that should be put in a marriage into the dating stages. Later they wonder why their husbands have been conditioned to sit back and let them do everything.*

Thought: *When women understand that men are the ones interviewing, not women, it allows a healthy structure to be established. Knowing this also establishes a sense of calmness in the women that will make them more desirable to men and less desperate.*

Flirt With Everyone You See

Once a friend whispered in my ear, "You flirt constantly with men." I looked at her and quickly denied it since I considered myself happily married for over two decades. After thinking about her comment, I became more aware of my actions with people. Soon enough, I realized that she was right. I do flirt with men, even though I am happily married. It was not until my friend mentioned it to me that I realized that I was actually flirting, even though I thought I was just being nice and making a special connection. A few months later I admitted to myself that not only do I flirt with men but I also flirt with women. I am just a flirt, to anyone, at any age, all the time.

After realizing what I was doing, I started having more fun with it and felt freer with it.

Flirting is an innocent way to make another person feel special and for someone to be at his or her best in every human encounter. In this concept, flirting does not include touching or saying intimate comments to the other person. I am talking about being extra friendly, being the first one to speak and saying hello to establish a connection. This is a vital attribute when you want to meet someone and it is also a great way to give each person the attention he or she deserves.

It is interesting how many people want to be more lovable but don't have a lovable personality. They refuse to smile, speak to others or go out of their ways to make someone else's day. Then they wonder why they are not treated special in their relationships.

Thought: *You can't help but win when the objective of flirting is not for intimacy but for a healthy connection full of respect and honor for another person. When this is the focus, then your flirting does not become gender based, because there is no ulterior motive. It just becomes a lifestyle change where you are simply taking the time to engage yourself with other people regardless of who they are and what they have to offer.*

Don't Twist His Arm

As we get older, we quickly start learning that we can't make anyone do anything that he or she does not want to do. Only in elementary school could a girl twist a boy's arm in the schoolyard and have him reluctantly do what she wanted him to do. Once we become adults the entire picture of making people do the things we want begins to change. *We can't keep people who don't want to be kept and we can't rescue anyone who doesn't want to be rescued. People can do what they want to do.*

If your mate doesn't want to willingly do something for you, do you really want him to still do it anyway? If you have to beg for him to marry you then it is obvious that he is not interested in marrying you. If he marries you when he really does not want to, your entire marriage will be reflective of being with a man who really doesn't want to be with you.

Thought: *It is so important not only to respect yourself, but also to respect your mate for you both to understand that he is a grown person. Regardless if he shares his ideas with you or not, he knows what he wants in life and it may or it may not include you.*

Harmless Comments Can Destroy

Women have the tendency to think that they know best. They know what's best for their children, friends and husbands. If they are honest with themselves, they think they know what is best for everyone whom they know. Many times women think they are helping their husbands or that their husbands need more structure and direction in their lives, but neglect to remember that these men were successfully living alone before they married. It is not uncommon for women to comment: "You need to go to the dentist or stop picking your nails or your belly is getting too big." Many times it is thought that the comments they make are harmless, honest and for their husbands' own good. But in reality, if these comments are repeated throughout the same day, a woman becomes a nag. If men were looking for a boss they would have married their bosses and if they wanted a mother then they still would be living at home.

Thought: *It is vital to learn to accept your mate just as he is without your personal opinion, input or judgment. If his attributes don't outweigh the things that bother you the most about him then either you are with the wrong person or you are so critical that no one could please you.*

Men Rarely Ask for Divorces

Most women don't realize that when they marry they usually have the ultimate say in whether the relationship lasts a lifetime or not. Women become the initiators until the very end. Men rarely ask for a divorce, but "two-thirds of all divorces are initiated by women."[1] Often, men are also unaware that their relationships are at a divorceable level. They usually think that things in the relationship are better than what they actually are. Men often feel that "things aren't that bad anyway." They are usually shocked and taken back when the "D" word comes up.

This same lack of motivation toward the marriage is represented in many ways. Men rarely initiate divorce but they also rarely initiate counseling, date night and communication. It just becomes part of their personalities. They often become comfortable being the receiver while the woman is the constant giver, even when it comes to divorce.

Thought: *When women begin to understand that they have the ultimate power to end a relationship, they see clearer the depth of control they have before, during and after the relationship.*

Find a Reputable Counselor

Sometimes a friend or family member can give good advice, especially if he or she has a healthy, strong and long-term relationship. But be careful what type of counsel and advice you allow in your life. When it comes to something as precious and serious as your marriage, it may be best to seek help from experienced and well referenced professionals or clergy. Your counselor should:

♦ Have the ability to look at both sides objectively and fairly.
♦ Be able to discuss the situation without emotions and antics but instead with facts, maturity and compassion.

♦ Feel comfortable being completely honest with you and free enough to speak the truth in your life, even though it might hurt you initially.

Thought: *A healthy and trusting relationship is one where you can also have one special person in your life with whom you can share the secrets of your relationship, both the good and the bad.*

You Can Still Respect Things You Don't Approve

A woman is not going to always approve of what her mate does and doesn't do. He is not looking for a mother to show him the way. Just because she doesn't approve of him skydiving because of safety issues does not mean that she cannot share in the joy of it. Sharing in his joy is just another way for a woman to connect with her husband. Just because it is not the right thing for the woman does not mean that it is not the right thing for him.

Thought: *In my experience in my relationship with my husband I try to base my fairness and approval on three basic questions. Consider them in your relationship:*

♦ Is he violating God?
♦ Is he breaking the law?
♦ Is he hurting anyone?

14

Forgive Yourself and Him

Why are so many women surprised and disappointed by their husbands? Unless a woman marries a con artist or a person with multiple personalities, the guy he was when she dated him is the same person that he will be after marriage. If he was not affectionate in the dating phase, why should you expect him to turn into Mr. Affectionate after marriage? Usually personalities and traits intensify after marriage. If he had an anger problem during the engagement, there may be more rage after the wedding. For you to expect something different from what he has already shown you is a reason for you to *forgive yourself*.

Forgive yourself for ever believing that you were so magical and influential that you could change and alter who he has developed into over years and years of his life experiences. I am not saying that people don't change and that we can't have an influence on others. However, if you did not transform him before the honeymoon the likelihood of changing him afterward is very unlikely. The problem is that too many women are so focused and eager to seal the deal with marriage that they actually don't see the signals that are right before them. They know their mates are not that helpful, sensitive or expressive early in the relationships but then they quickly decide that things are not so bad and they can "fix" their mates.

However, circumstances before the marriage drastically change after the vows. There is definitely less stress and less responsibility in a relationship before walking down the aisle. Life is easier without children, two careers, a mortgage or a mother-in-law. Although a woman is not able to tell exactly how a partner will be on a daily basis when children and other life challenges are involved, if she opened her mind and analyzed what she sees during the dating stage she would have had a pretty accurate idea. The signs are there the majority of the time when a woman meets a man. In cases where women preferred not to see, it becomes more of their fault than their husbands' fault when women expect men to change into something and someone different than they were before marriage.

Men often complain about how their wives have changed after the marriage. They talk about how their wives never wear makeup anymore or dress up to go out with them. It is also not uncommon for a man to talk about how his partner worked at being sexy to get his interest and catch him and then once she had him she started looking disheveled. I always tell men that if when they go to their girlfriends' houses and their girlfriends are consistently dressed down with messy hair then more than likely this is how their partners will continue to dress after marriage.

Women tend to think that their mates have changed as well, but more often than not women's desires and perspectives have done the most changing. They have changed due to the increase of responsibility, personal maturity and overall need. Because women often feel the heaviness and pressure of personal responsibility, women grow up quickly. They do it because they have to and feel they have no choice. Remember: *Who a person is before the marriage is only magnified after the marriage.*

As mentioned earlier, women need to *forgive themselves* for expecting their husbands to transform into "Prince Charming" after marriage when in actuality women should expect their husbands to be the very best they can be. That is all that women can fairly ask for: to expect the best that their husbands will ever be able to give to them. Women need to establish that their husbands take responsibility in the most efficient way that they can do it as long as the chores are accomplished. A woman would not like it if someone told her how to be a wife and mother. Women would be outraged if another person discounted what they were doing and called it wrong just because their approaches were different.

Women need to *forgive themselves* for assuming that their husbands understand what they are talking about when they talk about imbalances and for thinking that their husbands are being difficult for the sake of being difficult. Many times women and men unfairly assume way too much about one another. If a woman is feeling most of the increased responsibility in the household it is very possible that her husband is feeling nothing and no increased burden. A lack of burden and stress on his part can also answer why he is confused about her constant complaints about him.

You are probably thinking: *I keep telling him that I need help* or *why can't he just open up his eyes and see all the stuff that needs to be done around here?* Both of these statements are fair and logical. But is it a possibility that your husband is simply afraid of changing and helping around the house in fear of more criticism that he can't do the task up to your standards? And if he does to try to do it the best way that he knows how, would it still cause argument and strife because you would redo it to your specifications? I challenge you to ask yourself how much of what you husband might be thinking may be actually true. Are you hard to please? Are you a nag and a complainer? Do you feel that you are the only one who can do it right? Even if a little of this describes you in the smallest way, forgive yourself. Forgive yourself for being too difficult to please, for not being fun and relaxed and for prejudging your husband's wrongdoings before he actually makes any mistakes. Because if any of these descriptions fit who you really are, it is simply because you are tired, frustrated and seeking more balance.

Mistaking Passion for Satisfaction

Many times women mistakenly think their frustration is coming from one area when it is really stemming from a much deeper place. Have you noticed that a bad guy can be 90 percent bad for us yet we will still want and chase after him because of the passion that he gives us?

We can feel satisfied in a relationship that should give us no satisfaction all because we have passion toward the person. *It is safe to say that passion is the relationship deceiver.* When we have passion it just seems that nothing is as bad or intolerable as it otherwise would be. A partner's mishaps are overshadowed by how sexually turned on his mate is. Women make the mistake over and over again of thinking that relationship unbalance comes from their husbands' laziness or lack of spiritual commitment. Maybe these are contributing factors, but the problem first developed through a lack of a passion. *The absence of passion allows women to see what they really have and what they are really dealing with, because when women do have passion it is likely that they are blinded by some of the truth behind their relationships.* A woman can be with a man who worships the ground that she walks on but when she lacks passion toward him she is not satisfied with the relationship regardless of how good he is to her. Many have found something wrong even when there was nothing wrong at all simply because of a lack of passion.

This idea of passion being deceptive is not necessarily a new idea or discovery. For both men and women who marry more than once in their lives it is not uncommon for their first spouses to be partners whom they want, desire and have passion with. When all of the passion gets out of their systems, these people realize the "realness" and importance of relationships and tend to marry partners who are "best" for them the second time. But when a woman marries for passion and nothing else, it can cause long-term turmoil in a relationship.

When there is an obvious problem in a relationship such as imbalance and other very damaging circumstances, the very first thing that seems to disappear is the passion. *Once the effect of the passion is gone then the relationship blinders are off and partners can see what they truly have.* The problem with this is because of the frustration with the lack of passion, there can be an overwhelming sense of attention on another problem instead of on the issue of lost passion. What happens is that a person is not usually aware that he or she is compounding two issues into one and that one issue is getting double the anger. This anger is usually put on someone else, like the husband.

Another problem that comes from having a lack of passion is one men can relate to and could probably fix. Men know they should do things such as change the oil in the car and take out the trash without being told. Although they do not want to hear the complaints about what they should do, they know deep down that they could do better. But it becomes more complex when a wife's anger is compounded and overemphasized because the thought of having sex with him disgusts her. When a husband wonders why his wife has built up anger and drama in her words, he may never quite understand how complex it has become and how it really might have more to do with the lack of passion.

Men also tend to choose women whom they desire for their first marriages and more practical mates for their second marriages. But men react differently when their passion diminishes. When they lose the passion they often become interested in someone else. They are more likely to deal in infidelity or increase their flirting. They are not as prone to point out the mishaps of their wives because men are not geared and wired that way. They are not usually interested in giving that type of attention to someone in whom they have lost interest.

Just because you lose passion for your mate does not mean that you don't still love your mate. You still can love, adore and respect your mate but lack passion for him.

Showing Your Worst

Male, female, old or young, the ones closest to us often get the worst of what we have to offer. Your family gets the person in the early morning hours when you are depressed and pushing yourself to get to work. Then in the afternoon they get the used up, abused, exhausted and frustrated person who returns home from work. The people who have the most meaning in our lives get the worst of us. Co-workers and the people with whom we associate every day, often people whom we barely know, usually get the very best of who we are. They get the polished personality, the smiles and encouraging words that should also be going to our families. *There are too many women who go from being passive at work, because they feel like they have to be, to being aggressive at home, because they feel like they need to be.*

Many give the people who are supposed to be of top value in their lives very little attention. People who don't deserve as much attention very easily end up receiving all one's energy and focus. Many times women are more forthcoming about how they feel and what they want in life to strangers than they do to their own husbands. It is no secret most people know that they have given the wrong amount of energy and consideration to outsiders. Women must forgive themselves for giving their best not to their loved ones but to others.

Husbands Who Take the Blame

Historically, being passive and not speaking up has been an ongoing communication mishap for most women. They have also been guilty of not being able to say "no" and for consistently taking on too much responsibility. Although many women become more confident with speaking up and saying no, too many battle this their entire lives. Many times women come home abused and frustrated because they feel like they have been taken advantage of by other people. Then when their husbands don't take out the trash they hear the frustration that stems from everyone who has been abusive to their wives all day. If women could learn the art of saying no and establishing boundaries in their lives, they would not have pent-up frustration that gets released on their families.

Many women who have a hard time saying no also suffer from low self-esteem and take on a victim position. *Forgive yourself for blaming your husband for other people taking advantage of you.*

Forgive Him

Whenever you are committed to someone on a daily basis it is likely that you need to be forgiven and he does also. One of the biggest mistakes that women make is *assuming* that he knows. Women assume that their mates know that they are frustrated; they assume that their mates know when they are unhappy. They wonder why their mates don't know to do chores without their verbal requests. In any important bond and relationship it is always best not to assume anything. It is only after a woman has gently and calmly spoken with her husband and told him specifically what he can do to make things more peaceful in the house that she has the right to complain if he slacks off. If a woman has yelled a request instead of saying it, all that a man may understand is that she was yelling, not the actual words. Don't assume anything.

Three Secrets to Forgiveness

- Forgive before he asks for it.
- Forgive him and really let go of it.
- Give him the same forgiveness that you hope to receive in return from him.

15

Is the Marriage Worth Staying?

M any women have asked the question, "Is it worth it?" It is hard when the problem is as complex as this one. There is no doubt you should leave if your relationship involves abuse or if you are involved in a crime against your will. In these cases the decision is clear: You must walk away from your situation. But when there are definite pros and cons, good days and bad days, it is harder to know what to do. Sometimes when the woman has outgrown her mate, there are clear and obvious advantages about him that lets her know he is a good man. Knowing that he is decent makes the decision to leave even more difficult.

Another dilemma that many women face is after considering and reflecting on their partners' deficits and comparing their partners to friends' spouses, women may decide that what they have is not so bad after all.

The stigma characterizing men as the breadwinners and "men of the house" is slowly diminishing. Although a man is always respected for working hard and supporting his family, society and the media have become more tolerant of different lifestyle options, such as stay-at-home dads and men who work from home. Like the role of men, the role of women is changing. Both sexes need to be more tolerant.

Advantages versus Disadvantages

This whole idea of leaving brings up different levels of stress, frustration and confusion because of the changes and adapting that will need to occur for you and the children if you do decide to leave. When the fact of outgrowth is just one of many more serious problems, like abuse, alcohol, sexual and other addictions, that exist, it is easier to walk away and accept your relationship as a learning experience. However, when you know that he is faithful, loyal, loving and an overall good husband and father, it is a much harder decision to make. I and many other counselors feel it is becoming harder to find available and quality men. The more mature you get the more you realize that whomever you end up with will also have plenty of flaws and concerns that will eventually be uncovered. Sometimes it can be more productive to scrutinize and work on problems you know and understand than to deal with a new person's flaws and defects. Thus the decision to leave must be deeply reflected upon and not made in haste or because you feel so tired you can't take it any longer.

Many of my clients who are dealing with troubled marriages and partners' shortcomings ask me for signs or questions that they can reflect on when they are considering leaving their relationships. Here are some important questions I suggest you ask yourself:

♦ When you analyze your husband's personality over the years, has he been fairly open and willing to change or is he stubborn, bullheaded and someone who always needs to be right, therefore compromise appears impossible? If he is generally open, willing to listen and not completely stubborn, is he then willing to work on the marriage and will he be open to adjusting his present thinking?

♦ What are the things that you liked about your husband before you married him? What was it that made him different and allowed you to believe that he was the one with whom you wanted to spend your life? Are those qualities still there, but perhaps buried under life's problems? This is similar to how the fun-loving personality you might have had before your marriage is also still there but hidden under your personal stress.

♦ Outside of the outgrowth, do you feel that your husband loves you still and would fight to keep the relationship? If you believe that he is willing to fight for the relationship, then maybe you have not given him reason to feel like he needs to make the effort because you have demonstrated that you will. Many times people are in a rut and it has become the norm to hear the partner complain. *If what you are doing is not getting what you want then you need to change what you are presently doing.*

♦ Do you think that if your husband was in a relationship with another woman that she would see him as a problem like you do? Do you think that possibly his nice qualities have become distorted to you because you are overwhelmed with what is not going right in your relationship? Just as I am sure that he has taken you for granted, I am sure that you have also taken him for granted. *It is very important to sometimes put ourselves in our spouses' places and imagine what our partners feel in order to truly be able to understand and appreciate the relationship.*

♦ Do you respect him as a father? Although he is not perfect do you feel that he adds to your children's lives?

Does being a good father add to the character of who he is as a person?

♦ Has your relationship really been that bad? Have you become fixated on what is wrong in the relationship and obsessed with what needs fixing? Because we are human beings, we fixate and focus on what is not going right; we can oftentimes have a whole lot of good things going on around us and we only see what is wrong. Many times the wrong that we see becomes magnified and emphasized depending on the other stressors in our lives. When I ask many of my clients, "What is it that you liked about him when you first met him?" it is hard and sometimes impossible for them to remember. The reason for this loss of memory is because women have become so burdened and overwhelmed with the problems and cares of their lives that all they can see is what affects them the most. *What affects them the most is usually what hurts them the most.*

♦ Do you feel that you might have contributed to the stressful situations in your life by making your life too hard when you really did not have to? Do you overextend yourself? Do you have a personal problem with saying no? Although we often complain, many times there is a personal high at staying overly busy and being overwhelmed. Women will often base their self-worth and value on these issues. They believe the busier they are the more effective they are. Women tend to hate what the outgrowth brings but there is definitely a reward element to it in adding to their self-images.

♦ Have you gained something from this outgrowth that results in feelings of power and authority? Are you willing to give up these feelings if you could have a renewed and improved husband instead? Sometimes we think we want

our mates to improve when actually we don't really want
what we think we want. Women have grown to enjoy the
power that outgrowing their husbands brings. Often,
women become insecure when and if their husbands finally
gets themselves together. It can be easier when women feel
that their mates are flawed and deficient. When men renew
and improve themselves, they have more personal power
and this can increase women's insecurities.

♦ Is there a part of you that feels sorry for your mate,
  because you know that he is a good man and you fear
  that his self-esteem has suffered from having you become
  more successful and outgrow him? *When you know that he
  has potential and deep down he is a good person, it is easy
  for love to turn into sympathy.* When a woman knows that
  she has a "good" man, it is easy to have the tendency to
  feel sorry for him. She feels badly about how she treats
  him and quietly wonders what he would do without her.
  When he is "no good", a woman often concludes that he
  is getting what he deserves.

♦ Do you believe that he has been faithful to you and that
  he really has committed to the relationship for the future?
  Sometimes it is easier to deal with a man whom you have
  outgrown than a man who just can't be faithful.

♦ Do you wonder if you are partly to blame because in the
  beginning of the relationship you effectively used your
  ability to make his life easier, increasing his attraction to
  you?

♦ Do you feel that although you have outgrowth problems
  you are better off with him than without him? Have you
  discovered that he does add some joy and happiness to
  your life? Although there are problems, which there will
  be in every relationship, perhaps it's better to be with
  him than without him.

- Is what he is giving to you any different from what it always has been? Has life in general just magnified in responsibility and stress?
- Do you think that you could ever forgive him and start over? This is key if you are going to salvage your relationship. If you cannot forgive and move on so that your disapproval will not constantly remind him of past mistakes, even after he has improved, it is only fair to release him and allow him to start over with someone else.

Two Key Questions

Two questions that will give you "right now" answers on whether you should leave:

1. If you knew that you would never marry or seriously date anyone in the future, would you be as motivated to leave your present marriage?

Your answer to this first question lets you reflect on whether you prefer to be alone for the rest of your life or go on with the same amount of hurt, frustration and anger that you presently endure. If you answer yes then this allows you to make your decision independent of your emotions.

2. If you were to leave your husband and you knew that in one year he would be remarried, in love, happy and about to start a new family with someone else, would you be as motivated to leave?

If you are so unattached from your relationship that you really don't care if he moves on and starts a new life with someone else, it is very clear that you have nothing left to give your present relationship. This question also allows you to look at the very worst-case scenario, consider it for your life and then make a decision without having future expectations of something better happening. It is sometimes just easier for men to move on. If he is as dependent as you think, then he will be quick to get involved with someone else.

Many times, women make the grave mistake of leaving their present relationships with the intentions of finding and marrying their dream mates. I believe, and my professional experience has shown, that when this is the prime motivator behind leaving a marriage, it is a poor reason to do so. If you are going to leave your husband because you have outgrown him, truly believe you have no more to give the relationship and need to get on with your life whatever the future holds, make this a slow, careful, rational choice. It is not wise to base such a major decision on a dream or a hope that your Prince Charming is still out there.

16

Dreaming of Leaving

L ooking at the divorce rate of many of our friends and family members, one quickly realizes that despite all of the relationship conclusions and suggestions out there, whatever experts are advising really does not matter, because it is not working. The divorce rate is at an all-time high and there is also an increase in the number of people choosing to remain unmarried. A person in a marriage full of bliss is not part of the majority but part of the minority. There are so many people facing divorce and the decision to move on, it is time to look at what happens when leaving is the best thing for you, your husband and your overall circumstance.

Contemplating Divorce versus Dreaming of Divorce
Contemplating a divorce and dreaming of a divorce are two entirely different energy forces. Contemplating a divorce means thinking about it sometimes. It suggests that a woman has thought about being alone or has played with the idea of

finding someone different in her life. It is usually something
that goes in and then goes out of her mindset. Usually the urge
to divorce is stronger at different times in a woman's life. When
a woman contemplates her marriage she tends to think about
it much more when her frustration and stress concerning the
marriage elevates. *The more stressed she is the more she tends to
latch on to the idea of divorce.* When things are going in a normal fashion she is not that absorbed with the thought.

Dreaming of a divorce is a much deeper energy. I have
heard many women say, "I think of a divorce every single day
and it literally is the one thing that absorbs my thoughts."
When things have gotten so bad that a woman has lost interest
in her relationship with her husband and is obsessed with the
whole idea of getting out and leaving, *it just might be time to
go.* When it is on her mind every single day there is, she is not
in a position to give her relationship a fighting chance.

◆ **She becomes obsessed with what her husband is not.**
When the idea of marriage reaches this stage a woman
becomes *obsessed with what her husband is not.* She is no
longer willing to look at what he contributes or what he
has to offer, even if in the smallest way, but becomes
obsessed with the idea of what he is not. When it reaches
this point a woman can't win and her husband does not
have a fighting chance.

◆ **The idea of him with someone else relieves her.** A
woman no longer cares what her husband is doing or
who he is doing it with as long as he is out of her house
and her life. When the relationship has reached the point
that she wishes he had another woman the relationship is
over.

◆ **She won't forgive or forget.** When a woman is at a
point that she simply can't or won't forgive and forget
then staying in the relationship becomes unfair to her

husband. He may live his life apologizing to her but it won't be enough for her. It is not fair to either partner to put energy into a doomed relationship.

♦ **Love turns to hate.** Many times what happens when a couple stays in a dead relationship longer than they should is that their love turns to hate. This is a dangerous situation for any relationship. The same energy that was put into loving the mate at the beginning of the relationship is the same energy used in hating the mate now.

If what is on your mind the most is escaping and rescuing your own self by leaving the relationship, it is impossible to be committed to saving the relationship at the same time. *Whatever is on your mind the most during the day guides your mindset for the entire day. When the idea of divorce accompanies all daily activities, it is time to leave.* Being obsessed with such a big decision will affect your entire communication style toward your husband, your children and other people in your social circle. When you are obsessed with divorce it will change your entire personality and perspective until you are actually divorced. Even though you will try not to allow it, it will affect who you are as a person and you perspective on life. *When things get to this point and there is an internal battle—a struggle every day that you wrestle with inside—and the idea of divorce is no longer a nightmare but instead a personal dream, it is time to go.*

Chronic Infidelity

Having a one-time affair is less complex than chronic infidelity. A good man can slip up during a long, committed relationship and still be good, decent and worthy of your love and respect. *But when you are dealing with chronic infidelity, you are dealing with a problem that is bigger than you and actually has nothing to do with you.* It is more than just being weak in the moment: it may involve sexual addiction or a strong need to be wanted by multiple women. It also may be a deep-seated fear of commitment or of growing older and feeling the need to hold on to his youth as much as possible. A woman will not be able to solve the problem because she is not the problem. *More importantly, it involves a different caliber of man. Having a husband who participates in chronic infidelity suggests that he is a playboy, no good and a person who might have deeper issues that may need professional attention.* When it is at this level it is not about the wife and she alone can't fix it. Many women feel that because they have not seen the chronic infidelity until later in their relationships or not until after the outgrowth was evident that the chronic infidelity is solely about the outgrowth. But if a woman is dealing with someone who is having chronic affairs, the act or the desire for the act has been hidden in the relationship all along. Regardless if the partner was participating in multiple sexual acts with other women or not, if he desired it, thought about it and fantasized about it, then he has successfully committed the act of infidelity emotionally before physically. When this happens there is nothing left in the relationship. More than likely the woman has misjudged the depth of her original relationship anyway. The mindset, motives and desires of chronic infidelity were there even before marriage, even if they did not manifest until after the marriage. What he has chosen is not marriage and a wife but instead a playboy lifestyle. The reality is that he should have never got married in the first place.

With chronic infidelity the husband is usually sorry that he got caught but not sorry for what he has done. His deceptive ways and playboy mentality still remain deeply rooted inside him. Because of this it is very unlikely that his need or desire to be faithful will increase any time soon. The healthiest option for a woman in this situation is to leave the relationship.

When things are at this level it is obvious that he has already chosen what he wants and he has shown who he truly is. When people show who they are, believe them the first time.

Abuse

While many women may say they will leave a relationship that involves abuse, the emotional connection complicates this type of situation. Even more difficult is when the abuse is not physical but emotional. Women become confused and have trouble identifying when emotional abuse is present. Women are unsure where they stand in the relationship and whether what they are experiencing is actually abuse when it is not physical.

Abuse, regardless if it is physical or emotional, is about control. When he is abusive he is trying to have a place, stand his ground and redefine his importance. It is his way of making his partner need him even if it is through fear and low self-esteem. When outgrowth is the issue, abuse is often the result of his low self-esteem and his way of not knowing how to fix the problem. It is not uncommon for emotional abuse to arise after outgrowth is established. *In many cases emotional abuse starts out as manipulation and it quickly develops into emotional abuse, which is controlling the situation by degrading and devaluing the other person.* It is not as common for physical abuse to appear due to outgrowth; this type of abuse usually appears early in a relationship through shoving, pushing and aggressive physical interaction. It is not really about what a woman does or how much she nags; it is more about a need for the partner to control. Emotional abuse often starts out as manipulation and then when the wife responds to the emotional abuse by listening or being quite, it tells the abuser that his method has successfully worked and that he should continue to do what he is doing.

When outgrowth is the reason for emotional abuse it is usually the only tool that a partner has left. It becomes the only thing at which he can successfully outdo his wife. In fact it is a cowardly way for him to establish himself as "the man." It is the one way that he can get and keep control.

Regardless if it is physical or emotional, abuse is the ultimate deceiver and a worthy reason to end a relationship. If a woman stays in an abusive relationship, the maze of the abuse will grow deeper and deeper until her self-esteem is so low that she will not recognize herself any longer.

His Low Self-Confidence

Low self-esteem is a much bigger problem than most people realize. It can be the hardest thing to overcome in a relationship. When a person feels that he has nothing to offer then a couple doesn't have much to work with in a marriage. It is almost impossible to make someone else love and respect his or her own self. *When a partner's confidence level is determined by whether a mate likes him, it creates strain on the relationship.* If a partner feels like he doesn't have anything to offer the relationship then he will not offer anything. If he feels he is pathetic and not worth anything then he will be exactly what he thinks.

The danger of having a man with low self-esteem is that eventually a woman will lose respect for him. She will not want him because he is more like a child than a mate with whom she can have a loving relationship. A mate with low self-esteem becomes like extra baggage weighing the other partner down and the other partner will resent him for not being his own person.

When a mate's self-esteem is this low, in most cases it is impossible for his partner to repair it. Regardless of how much a woman assures her mate that he is enough, if he has this type of issue then the effort will be worthless. "Nice guys" are often haunted by low self-esteem and self-doubt. Their wives wish they would not be so nice and toughen up instead, leading them to doubt themselves. Many times low self-esteem is an indication that a man married "out of his league" and doesn't feel he can contribute to the relationship. Other times a man may have low self-esteem due to other issues in his life and may need professional counseling to overcome this problem.

Low self-esteem can lead a partner to become bitter. He resents the fact that his mate has a healthy self-confidence. This may not be visible in the relationship, because his lack of confidence prevents him from showing how he truly feels. But a man with low self-esteem tends to grasp and hold on to anyone who will protect, nurture and provide, both financially and emotionally. Regardless of the source of the need, it is usually a problem that mates are not equipped to fix. Instead of having a husband, a woman feels she has a dependent child. When this is the case the relationship is over.

"No Good" Men

Women often are attracted to the very thing that causes problems later. They often want the good-looking, smooth-talking man whom all the other women want too. But this type of man is usually full of danger and women are too smitten to see it.

Some men are simply no good. These men feel they are the prize and a gift to women. They enter a marriage with one foot in and the other foot out the door. No good men expect women to be happy simply for the fact that they married them. At the same time, these men feel the need to continue asserting their player sides. They constantly try to get the attention of other women and enjoy it. They don't consider their mates' feelings. Women have to face the fact that sometimes they are not good judges of character and make bad choices. Some women marry whom they want instead of whom they need.

When a relationship is haunted by this demon, the woman needs to admit that she made a mistake and should not have married him. A relationship like this is not healthy and will not last. Women must learn to forgive themselves, pick up the pieces and move on with life. *The next time a woman coming from this situation considers marriage she should consider what she needs and allow what she wants to be secondary.*

17

Looking for a New Mate

Although we know that it only makes sense to want the very best for ourselves, sometimes what we are attracted to is simply not what we need.

Dangerous Men
Is it true that dangerous men and women are more attractive than "good" ones? For some people it is. They have a pattern of picking the same type of "bad" person over and over again. When women have this problem, more often than not it is more about the insecurity and the desperateness of the woman than the man.

Here are some red flags that are usually present when you are dating a person who is emotionally dangerous from author Sandra Brown's book *How to Spot a Dangerous Man Before You Get Involved*:[1]

♦ You feel uncomfortable about something he has said or done, and the feeling remains.

- You think you are the only one who can help/love/understand him.
- You feel bad about yourself when you are around him.
- You feel he wants too much from you.
- You tell friends you are "unsure about the relationship."
- You feel isolated from other relationships with family and friends.

Some dangerous men may seem "too good to be true" and often are. They are talented chameleons, changing their personalities from environment to environment and focusing on pleasing whomever is present at the moment. In a relationship, a dangerous man may claim an immediate connection with you—one that you may not believe or reciprocate—and share personal information or emotions too early in the relationship and push you to do the same.

Dangerous men have a need to be right and will do whatever they can to prove they are right. This type of man may also be clingier in the relationship than is healthy. Even though a dangerous man may seem charming, you or others may notice something a little off about the relationship. You may find you make excuses for yourself and to your family and friends as to why you are in the relationship.

It is important to mention that a person doesn't have to be a criminal to be dangerous. A dangerous person, male or female, is simply someone who is unhealthy to be around and therefore brings that same unhealthiness into a relationship.

Brown says there are several types of dangerous men:[2]

- **The Man Who Clings Too Much:** Many women feel as though they can't breathe when in a relationship with this type of man and often feel these men drain them of energy and life.

- **The Man Who Expresses Violence:** When a woman feels that she has to walk on eggshells every day and she is not sure what type of mood her mate is going to be in when he gets home, often she is in the beginning stages or a progressive level of abuse.
- **The Man Who Struggles With Addiction:** It is often difficult for men to hide addictions, but they will quickly deny that they are addicted.
- **The Man Who Preys On Emotions:** This person is a con artist and when a woman bases her actions on her emotions, she is an easy target to pursue and string along. It is best not to trust people who feel like they know you too quickly, unless they are professional therapists.
- **The Man Who Needs A Parental Figure:** Most women have a hard time respecting this person because they want more for themselves. Women get caught up in rescuing men like this, which give them a lot of personal power.
- **The Man Who Has A Secret Past:** Usually a woman has a sense that something is not right or that there is something in the man's past that she doesn't know, but she often dismisses the idea and figures she is simply being paranoid.
- **The Man Who Is Mentally Unhealthy:** Many times, unless we have been trained in the area of mental illness, we are hesitant about making diagnoses and find it uncomfortable that we wonder if someone is emotionally ill. Sometimes women feel paranoid or are accused by their mates of being "off" themselves. Fear, uncertainty and the desire to save him can make a woman a victim of a man who is mentally ill.
- **The Man Who Guards His Emotions:** Many women are very "turned on" by this type of person because he becomes a personal challenge and so the relationship remains on an uncertain basis for a long time.

Delaying Marriage

In everyday life and in Hollywood it is not odd to see men dating for longer periods and marrying at older and more seasoned ages. Good examples of this are George Clooney and Hugh Hefner, both well-known celebrities. It is not uncommon for popular male celebrities not to parade the fact that they are married. It is part of the attraction for the rest of us to feel that he is available and that we actually might have a chance. This tendency to hold out also resides with everyday people. It is not uncommon to see the most popular boy in college holding off falling deeply for one girl or getting too serious with anyone in fear that he might lose his popularity. It is becoming less rare to see a good looking hunk wait until he is in his early sixties to be ready to settle down.

Living together instead of getting married is also a growing trend. The number of unmarried partners living together is skyrocketing. Until recently, it was scandalous for an unmarried man and woman to live together. Couples found themselves attacked by angry family members, excluded from faith communities, baffled by how to introduce each other and discriminated against because they were not married. This negative reaction is quickly fading and today, most couples who marry live together first—"shacking up" has gone mainstream.

Some couples find living together the easy and most economical way. It is interesting that in some places and situations, unmarried partners can share a health insurance policy and get certain legal protections; in other states, they're considered legal strangers with no rights, even if they've lived together for decades. A lot depends on the conservatism of the state and local protocol of the city.

Sex before Marriage

In the past, when the older and baby boomer generation were dating, there were more marriages and commitment to long-term relationships. There has been a steady decline in the need for formal commitment and infidelity. I believe sex before marriage has not helped this cause. Waiting until marriage to have sexual relations causes the relationship to be built on other important factors besides sex such as friendship, acceptance and conditional love. These relationship attributes can carry the relationship if there are sexual problems or if sex decreases or stops due to illness or other factors.

As discussed in chapter 2, it very common for sex to happen in the liking stage. It can be a long-term hardship for the relationship because it establishes a belief that intimacy is sex and sex is intimacy. So many women have sex without intimacy early in the relationship and then later in the courtship want to be held, be cuddled and experience the joys of affection, when all along what they truly desired most was the full satisfaction of intimacy. Instead of having sex so quickly in the relationship, in order to produce a stronger relationship in the long-term, it is best to first master the intimacy and establish the beauty of that before sexual relations. Not only do adult men and women not understand the concepts of sex and intimacy but also parents and society have done a poor job of teaching children the unique value in each one of them.

When sex is initiated early in the relationship it usually means different things to both the man and the woman. Although things are changing, for many women having sexual relations means a deeper level of closeness, a new level of emotional discovery and that the partners belong to each other exclusively. There are exceptions, but for many men it means just the opposite. Once women consent to sexual intercourse, men's mission has been accomplished, conquest has been achieved and unless the women are really special, there really is no deeper level of discovery needed or reason for the relationships to continue. Now this does not mean that the man can't continue to be interested in the woman, but in too many cases he seems to lose interest after the first sex. In fact, the emotional closeness that the female begins to feel through sex is an automatic turnoff for many men. Instead of feeling especially close, he starts detaching emotionally. Often women try harder and harder, desperate to establish a closeness that does not exist and men pull away.

There are definite signs that women can look for to help protect them from this relationship pitfall. *There is usually false truth before sex and the real truth comes after the sex.* If when a woman meets a potential mate he says "sweet sayings" to her that are too good to be true, then they probably are. Some of the common phrases are: "You are the most beautiful woman I've ever seen; I am surprised you are single; you understand me more than any woman in my past relationships." When a woman first meets someone and he utters these clichés, she should assume that he has said the same lines to many women before. If on the second date he confesses that he has never felt this way toward any other women, in many cases, he is trying to lure the woman into the bedroom. Over exaggerated words in the very early stages of the relationship is a clear sign that a potential mate's intentions are shallow. But if that mate knew the future destruction and hurt that his empty words bring, he would not be so quick to use them. Such strong emotions are rarely developed just after meeting someone for the first time. When someone says words that suggest you are the most beautiful being who has ever existed or that his life began the day he met you, it is best to assume that there is an ulterior motive, which is usually sex.

Another good way to judge the character of a mate is to observe how patient and understanding he is when it comes to not having sex initially. Some people are motivated to wait due to the possibility of their mates having sexually transmitted diseases. Some people require their mates to get tested before sex. It is wise to make sure that you and your mate are not carrying any type of sexual transmitted disease. It is much too trusting to assume that a stranger is clear and free of any such disease. *When you sleep with a person you are also sleeping with every person with whom he ever had sex.* Does your mate care enough about you to ensure your comfort in this area? Is he mature enough to truly comprehend the importance and value of getting tested for both his protection and yours? Being willing to get tested before sex does not ensure that you have a mate worth keeping, but it does suggest that the other person has nothing to hide and that there is a certain level of maturity about a potentially serious relationship.

Another way that waiting to have sex shows a mate's true purpose is his reaction to your telling him that you don't believe in sex before marriage, if this is true for you. The reaction of your mate will determine the character and the intentions of your mate toward you. It is one of the fastest ways to see if his ethical values match yours. In most cases, the reason for abstinence before marriage is religious. Of course there are exceptions to this rule: Some people desire to share their sexual experience solely with their spouses. Some people practice abstinence for safety and cleanliness reasons. Despite the reason why, those couples who decide to wait until they are married before they have sex many times develop a relationship built from friendship.

This topic of sex usually becomes open for discussion in the liking stage. And when the one mate mentions to the other that she is interested in practicing no sex until marriage one of three things usually occurs. The first reaction and most likely response is that the mate will try to convince his partner to reconsider her beliefs and have sex. He will usually try to convince her that they will be together for a long time, so why wait? When the other mate does not have the same moral convictions and same religious beliefs, it is most common for him to try and convince his mate to rethink her decision. He will repeatedly say that this relationship is more special than the others or he will assure his mate that he will be gentle. Many times, people will try to convince their mates that if they really cared for them they would allow intercourse to happen. The mate will usually try for a period of time to convince his partner to give in. If the partners are still not willing to conform after a few weeks many people choose to walk away and abandon the relationships. Walking away doesn't suggest that the mate does not care for the other person, but many times the person wanting intercourse doesn't feel that the relationship is worth waiting it out. He doesn't see his mate as a future spouse, so to suggest that there will be no lovemaking until marriage seems completely foolish.

The second most common reaction is that the mate will often leave the relationship. The obstacle of not having sex brings on too much drama and friction for a relationship just starting out and the opposing viewpoints may not be worth it. Some people will leave almost immediately and others will quietly fade out of the picture. The person who desires sex will often see no other reason for continuing the courtship if sex is not involved. He knows that it would be very easy to have a successful relationship with sex with someone else, so he feels there is no reason to deal with a mate who does not feel the same in this area. After the partner discloses her desire to have no sex, when the mate's sole reason for being with that person is sex, the other person will disappear from the woman's life. The person will start being unavailable and uninterested.

Finally, there are a few very special people who are willing to conform to the desires of their mates and also wait until marriage. It is always very special when a woman finds a mate who is willing to share her same belief system when it relates to no sex. *In order for this decision to be successful, it is imperative that the couple find other meaningful experiences they can share together.* This could be the act of friendship, a shared religious belief or just a strong desire to respect the wishes of each partner. It has been proven that when a couple is willing to wait until marriage before intercourse that there develops a special trust and appreciation between the two people. Their courtship along with their marriage tends to be bonded with a specialness that is only shared by two people with the same goal. To know that your mate is willing to wait until marriage before sex usually means that commitment in the courtship is achieved at a faster rate. In actuality, not only commitment, but also friendship, discovery, proposal and marriage tend to happen quicker because it is realized sooner in the relationship that each mate is someone very special and worth keeping.

If remaining celibate until marriage is important to you, it is imperative to find a mate who either shares in your beliefs or is willing to conform to how you feel. If you settle in this area and give in because you have a mate who is just not willing to wait, it is likely that you will easily settle in other vital areas in your life. When a partner is not willing to wait for sex, the challenge of getting you into the bedroom becomes the most important thing. It is what he is most consumed with. Caring, friendship and even love become secondary. Your body becomes a personal mission. Every word that is said and every date that you go on is for the sole reason of exploring you sexually. That is the reason why when most women give into the idea of intercourse before marriage, it is not uncommon for them to become fearful that their mates will quickly lose interest.

Today's Women Can Do It Themselves

I feel it is a positive advancement that women are more self-sufficient and able to support themselves in this era. This definitely has brought a more creative and interesting female to the surface. One who is a more independent thinker, competitor in the workforce and mother who learns to multitask to balance home and work. Many experts would agree that it was not until the disappointment and the breakdown of the family did the female feel a need to readjust, rethink and become a more sufficient individual. Although the whole notion of women working allows for fewer stressed men as well as more confident women and children who are exposed to more progressive lifestyles, this new mindset has also lessened the need for the more traditional man. *If the woman can support herself, why does she need him?*

For many women, now their relationships are building on authentic love only. The need for a man to support the family has steadily decreased and is not as much a priority. It has caused women to be more particular about their choices and it has caused men to be more liberal about theirs. The women's liberation movement has many advantages but it has also caused a need for the man to redefine his role in the woman's life. *Women added to what they can offer to the family and this caused a lack of clarity and meaning in men's lives.*

The same independence goes for the man. If he is able to run the house, handle the kids and work and support his family at the same time, there is less overall need for a woman. The ability of both sexes to multitask makes them very valuable to themselves and to their families. But it adds to them being stressed, overworked and misunderstood.

Can Faith Save Our Relationships?

Those who have strong religious faith feel that faith establishes boundaries and oftentimes defines what they will and will not do. For many it becomes their conscience, their ethics system and their measuring stick of what they determine as right and wrong.

I believe as human beings we have made a grave mistake focusing on what we should not do as it pertains to our faith instead of emphasizing what we could do and should do because of it. For many of us our faith tells us that we should marry so that we are committed to one and not multiple people. Our faith tells us we should wait before having sex because the act itself is so precious that it should be shared with only two people who are formally joined. Our faith tells us to forgive our husbands when they are not doing their parts around the house and to gently teach and be patient with them. However, for those of us with faith it also tells the husband to help the wife without being asked, because he loves her and does not want her overworked, stressed or unhappy.

When faith is strong enough it will challenge us to consider the needs of others before our own. When our faith is strong enough we don't get angry and fume over things and situations as quickly. More temperance and patience is usually developed. Often, when people of faith marry their mates they understand that they are not perfect and that their mates will never be. When a couple has great faith, their supreme joy and peace comes from their relationship with God, so they are very clear that they can't and will not find perfection in each other. This allows a spouse to realize that a partner will make mistakes and it allows each partner to be human, which can lead to a more successful relationship. This whole concept of giving up control and looking at the needs and desires of a partner tends also to be easier for those who have a stronger faith.

Giving Up Control

Two important factors for marriage success are "the man's ability to accept influence from his partner" and "the woman's ability to moderate her approach to seeking influence."[3] It is the personal decision of each partner to forfeit control in a relationship. When both mates acquiesce, the relationship can thrive.

Partners must respect and consider each other's viewpoints. Discussions should be started calmly and positively. Perhaps mutually agreeing on a time or schedule to talk could give both partners time to consider and work through emotions.

Compromising

Many times we go into relationships expecting to change the people from who they are to what and whom we want them to be. But people rarely change. What you get before the marriage will more than likely elevate and escalate after the relationship. It is best to decide on two or three things in a relationship that you "must have." It is popular for many women to desire:

♦ A successful man
♦ A person who is physically fit and takes care of himself
♦ Someone who is spiritual and connected to God

It is best to pick two or three things that you feel are necessary, stick with them and don't settle; then be willing to work with the rest. Experts have often said that you have a successful start if you can get 80 percent of what you want and are willing to work with the other 20 percent, as long as you have the "must haves" you are seeking.[4] It is also important to remember that your mate will have a "must have" list also; this goes both ways.

Revealing Introductions

There are so many small signs that we neglect to see in our partners that reveal so much about the quality of relationship we have. When we accurately learn to detect them we can quickly answer the mysterious commitment questions that we have.

So much is revealed in an introduction. How a man feels about a woman and the role she is really playing in his life will be demonstrated in how he introduces her. If he introduces a woman as his friend to others then that is exactly how he sees her—as a friend. Oftentimes, he will be more honest in his introduction than with his partner. *Now, the ultimate level of truth is how he introduces and talks about you when you are not around.* For example, if a woman enters a library and while waiting outside her partner meets some friends and he casually mentions "my fiancée just went into the library", that truly tells his level of commitment to the relationship. When a woman is not around and he still refers to her as his fiancée, it is a good sign.

Thought: *When he is truly committed to you he will not want to hide you.*

When Something's Wrong with Every Guy

It is not uncommon for women to become so critical and guarded that they find fault in every man they meet. He is not successful, he is a slob or he still lives at home with his mother are some of the popular excuses women tend to make. Even in the smallest thing some women have the tendency to criticize and find fault.

It is a sign when a woman can't find anything good in any of the men she meets. It is easier on a woman's ego to simply make excuses and never know that possibility of love than to realize that she simply is not loveable. *When women are critical and negative with every man they see it is usually a reflection of the negativity that they feel about themselves.* Many times women just don't feel loveable. They really don't believe that any man of quality would want to be with them for the long-term. They see their strong personalities as problems and curses and believe the fact that they know what they want out of life is seen as being inflexible and stubborn.

Thought: *Too often is it easier never to give love a chance than to believe in it and have it fail anyway.*

Want Versus Need

Because women are human beings they are looking for the best men they can find. Women want the smartest, most attractive and most successful people they can possibly find.

Some women tend to base opinions on what they see and pretend that that is all there is to a person when this is not the case. Usually the one who proves to be the best one for us and the one who will love us unconditionally is the one in whom we are usually initially interested. This usually happens because a man's biggest quality is not what is seen physically, but what is on the inside. But women have the tendency to base what they want on what they see and oftentimes overlook the men they should have.

Through observation it seems that men who are high school graduates, have good and reliable jobs and are not necessarily drop-dead gorgeous are often the ones who make the most steadfast and loving husbands. These tend to be the men most women overlook. After searching for Mr. Right for years it is easier to overlook than to reassess priorities and what is actually important in a man. After years of not finding the men whom they think they want, perhaps women should look harder at the other men whom they casually overlooked.

Thought: *Although you want to have passion in your relationship, you might have more relationship success by considering the man who is the most smitten with you instead of the one with whom you are most smitten.*

Allow Him to be a Man

Recently I was talking with Jackie, a client, and she felt a need to spend less time with her present boyfriend, William, because they were spending every waking day with each other. Although Jackie had a strong need to have more time to herself, she never brought the idea up to William, because she feared she would lose him. The day after our appointment, William called Jackie and said that he felt they should start seeing each other three or four times per week instead of every day. After her phone call with him Jackie immediately called me, because she felt that he was trying to break up with her. My response to her was "allow him to be normal and allow him to be honest with you." What William asked of Jackie is secretly what she wanted anyway, but because he had the nerve to bring it up instead of her, it made her feel insecure. How unfair, because she was setting him up to fail, without even knowing it.

Thought: *Usually when a woman's expectations are so unrealistic that her mate could never meet them, it is usually a reflection of her low self-esteem and a fear of not being able to keep the relationship.*

The Myth of Excitement

Too many women are waiting for Prince Charming to come and whisk them off their feet into romantic heaven. They want all of the positive attributes they desire to be present all at once. Most women want their mates to be gorgeous, rich, faithful and exclusively into them.

Many people believe that the man of your dreams must excite you the very first time. From my coaching experience I have realized that usually the one with whom a woman is the most thrilled and smitten is oftentimes the one who is the worst for her. When women are smitten and excited, it is often over the wrong things—things that will often sidetrack them from what they really should be looking for. It usually has very little to do with a man's quality, integrity or ability to make a woman happy on a long-term basis. Women are usually excited about men's looks, cars or muscles, which are all outside factors. What they should be excited about are the inside factors such as honesty, loyalty, spiritual connection or belief in family and commitment. When women are initially excited by men, it is important to realize that those feelings of being in "awe" will fade and the more normal and real person will quickly come to the surface.

Thought: *Passion is an important thing to have in any intimate relationship but it is not a reliable emotion on which to build a long-term relationship. Passion will fade as soon as trust, loyalty and commitment start fading away.*

When "Living Together" is About Fear

Because living together has become so common, women often will hide behind the practical side of living together instead of unraveling the truth. Yes, it could be a trial marriage to see if mates can effectively work through conflict. Yes, living together is less expensive and a way to plan for the future. The answer is yes, living together definitely has its benefits. But when the desire to live together is more one-sided and it is the woman who does most of the convincing and the pushing, there is definitely a problem. Here are the top three hidden reasons why women tend to want to live with their mates:

1. Many times the woman feels that her boyfriend will not propose on his own. Because the next likely step after living together is marriage, she becomes convinced that he is more likely to propose when he sees that they can successfully live together.

   If a boyfriend has to be coerced to propose, he is simply not ready for the commitment. If the marriage does happen, he will more than likely go through his entire relationship wondering if he did the right thing and wondering what his life would be like single. The likelihood of the relationship being healthy, happy and long-term is poor.

2. Many times, a woman is more likely to want to live together when she fears that her mate might date someone else. It is much easier to keep tabs on him when he comes home to her every night.

   In reality, if a mate is going to cheat, there are a lot of opportunities for him to do so. Even though he may be in bed with his partner at night, he can be playing the field during the day. To build a relationship with someone whom you don't trust is very unwise. There are reasons for your lack of trust and it stems from either him or you: him because he is not trustworthy or you because of insecurity. Regardless of who is to blame, when you don't trust him *before* you marry him, it is almost impossible to have a healthy future.

3. In some cases a woman doesn't believe her partner is capable of living on his own.

   If a man can't live independently before a marriage, he is not ready to commit to marriage. He will just become a burden to his partner and will be unable to pull his weight in the relationship. More than likely the woman will be the one carrying the load throughout the entirety of the relationship. This "handholding" period will eventually grow to become resentment.

Premature Planning

Women make a grave mistake by taking the fun out of dating. To them, everything has to be so serious. If men really knew the obsession that happens with many women just after one date, they would avoid women. Many times, by the first date the woman has wondered if he is the one. She has told all her friends about him and she may have already daydreamed of having his baby. Premature planning is a deadly mistake. When a woman is caught up in the serious side of a relationship, it is hard to just flow, have fun and enjoy the ride. His mind is usually so far from anything like marriage. When the woman starts the relationship with emotions and commitment, the relationship begins imbalanced.

Male or female, people are always disappointed when their plans don't work out. In this case, every successful phone conversation and every solid date just reinforces the woman's premature planning even more. The dream of a wedding, marriage and children becomes more and more believable to her.

Dating Will Not Cure Loneliness

Loneliness causes people to do a lot of negative things that do not bring companionship and fulfillment. It is not only a form of being alone and not wanting to be, but also a personal sign that there is something missing from life and that something is extremely wrong. *We often are deceived in thinking that loneliness is an outside problem, but in actuality it has everything to do with the inside of you.* In contrast, being alone is an outside manifestation that can be satisfied with another person.

There is a big difference between being alone and lonely. Being alone means just that. *Today you are sitting alone in your home sipping your coffee.* Loneliness is the negative feeling that you have about being alone. It is how you feel. *I am lonely today. I wish I had a date.* In order to have a successful marriage it is wise to get comfortable with being alone before the actual marriage—to be happy, content and fine with being by yourself. When you are seeking someone to come into your life and fix an internal feeling that you have inside of you, it is asking a whole lot from your partner who also has personal issues he is dealing with himself. *If you are not whole before you meet him, you will not be whole after you marry him.* Now, can a marriage stop you from being alone and depressed, so often? Probably, but the fact that you are seeking someone to fill up a void that you should be filling up yourself is not only unwise but also unfair. Again, no one person could ever be your knight in shining armor for every situation all the time. When we get in the habit of looking for someone to fulfill or satisfy what we need to complete by ourselves, it simply results in eventually being alone or having an unhealthy and unhappy relationship.

When you can prove to yourself that you can be alone without being lonely you are on your way to being whole. Some people treasure the times when there is no one else around and they can simply relax. Many people who are emotionally strong still suffer from loneliness from time to time, but when loneliness becomes a disorder and a major complaint then it is likely that the problem lies within you. A fellow therapist once made a very telling comment: "If I have to be alone, I am not a bad person to grow old with."

Putting Your Mate on a Pedestal

Women need to realize quickly that regardless of how a man is packaged on the outside there is a whole lot that they are unaware of on the inside.

Sara, who is a forty-four-year-old licensed attorney, has three kids ages ten to twenty-one. Although Sara has had a mental breakdown in the past and has ADD issues, she is on medication that helps her function normally. Until recently, Sara went five years without a serious date and although she wanted a man in her life, she was fairly content going to work and taking care of her sons. In our conversations I noticed how whenever Sara met a potential date she instantly became obsessed with him. For example, she saw a coach at her son's baseball game whom she found attractive and she started videotaping without his knowing it. She dreamed about him at night and fantasized about them being intimate, often interrupting her work.

All this thought and energy happened with the coach before she ever even knew his name. Sara knew nothing about him; she did not know if he was married, engaged or even interested in her. This silent love affair went on for a couple of months. She never approached him or asked his name, but she assumed that he liked her too, because she casually saw him looking in her direction once or twice during games. Sara started shopping every Monday before practice to buy sexy outfits to get his attention on the ball field and she also waited around after practice hoping that they would finally talk. She really believed in her head that he had the same interest in her and she convinced herself that he was simply playing a game with her.

After a few months Sara finally decided to approach him and made it clear that she was open to having sex with him and spending some "quality" time together. The coach was open to the possibilities and asked her out on a date. After the first date they slept together and he left for home the following morning. Sara expected to get a call to discuss their next date but the coach never called. She assumed that he lost her number so she anxiously called him. After many attempts to call, she decided to look him up on the Internet and drove to his home address. When she arrived at his house she saw him outside with his wife and two small children.

At baseball practice the next week, Sara approached the coach and asked him why he did not tell her about his wife and kids. He very calmly explained, "You never asked. You did not ask me anything about my life or my present relationships, so I figured that you did not want to know." He mentioned that he would have told her everything had she inquired and explained that he and his wife had an "open" relationship where they were allowed to date and have sex with other people as long as they didn't fall in love. After hearing this Sara was crushed. She blamed the coach because she thought he was deceitful, but ironically she neglected to blame herself for putting him on a pedestal.

Sara had known nothing about the coach. The only thing that she knew for sure was that she was attracted to him. For months she had a secret emotional affair with him and within that time she built up trust, hope, lust and infatuation. She had already started dreaming about their wedding day. She assumed that he was decent, unmarried, available and interested in her before she knew his name. Women make a grave mistake in assuming too much and too fast about their potential mates. The only thing that they can be sure of is that the men exist and are living and breathing—anything else is an assumption.

18

Release or Rekindle?

Depending on personality, tolerance level and past experiences, couples determine when to make decisions at different times of their lives. People are different and what is right for one person is not necessarily right for another. It is not uncommon for the tolerance level of a no-nonsense wife to be quicker, thus she will make a faster decision about her long-term relationship than someone who is more passive. *The more outspoken a woman is the less willing she will be to suffer increased marital drama for an extended amount of time.*

It is also important to recognize that the more bold and outspoken a woman is the less likely she is to get in a situation where she has completely outgrown her husband. It can and does happen, but in many cases she is more likely to acknowledge the signs of imbalance early in the relationship. In the past, even when imbalance was present in the marriage the couple was much more likely to endure the problem simply because it was discouraged and divorce was not popular.

Because many women saw their relationships as "no way out commitment" they were less likely to express or be deeply introspective about their real feelings, even when they knew that the relationship was lacking, unhappy or, even worse, abusive. Since divorce was infrequent women had to hang in and deal with day-to-day life.

The issue of whether to stay or leave most often comes from the woman. *Although many times a woman doesn't realize the magnitude of her own power, she is the one who determines the start and finish of everything significant in a relationship.* Women start out having all the power, though many give it over to men out of sheer desperateness. The woman is the "yes" person. *She decides if the relationship will begin at all and she determines if and when the relationship will end.* Often the woman will give over her power and start pursuing a man instead of allowing herself to be pursued. She gives up the number one power that she has: the ability to say yes.

Remember, statistically it is *rare for a man to ask for a divorce*. It does happen now more than it did in the past, but usually if a relationship stops the "no", in most cases, comes from the woman. Even in the case of infidelity, the husband might be interested in having an extra woman on the side, but he will rarely leave his present wife for his lover.

Regardless if you decide to release or rekindle your relationship there has to be somewhat of a mutual understanding between you and your partner, since in most relationships there is usually a form of imbalance in the decision making process—one person wants to either release or rekindle the relationship more than the other.

Regardless of who wants what, it is vital that the two parties are at least on the same page and that one partner does not want something completely different than the other. If the wife wants to release and the husband is hoping to rekindle, the wife will resent her husband for holding her back and the husband will feel that it should not have come to this.

It is hard to convince a person to stay when she or he has made up her or his mind to go. *In most cases, when two people obviously disagree whether to move forward or to end the relationship, the one who wants to release the relationship tends to work harder on getting what she or he wants.* The person who wants to rekindle will oftentimes verbally express hope for the relationship but unfortunately will not try in other areas to fix the problem. *If the person wanting the relationship knew how to please her or his mate in the first place, she or he more than likely would not be in the present circumstances.* The person is at an extreme disadvantage by not knowing how to please the spouse and now having resistance. She or he now has a spouse who has given up and lost hope in the relationship.

The partner who wants to stay is dealing with a deeper problem because she or he has to cope with resentment, hopelessness and rejection. If this partner could not win over the love of the spouse when both were trying to make the partnership succeed, it is impossible to convince the other spouse when she or he has already made up her or his mind to move on.

When one wants to release and the other wants to rekindle, in most cases the one who has the desire to release wins and gets his or her way. The reason for this is because the mate who wants to rekindle will usually give up hope and feel that there is no possibility to reconcile or the person who wants to release makes life so unbearable that after a while the other spouse gives in.

Whether a couple decides to release or rekindle the relationship, the reason behind both decisions is the same: forgiveness. *They "release" the marriage because of a lack of forgiveness and they decide to "rekindle" the marriage due to the ability to forgive.* The act of forgiveness determines the final decision that the couple decides to make. Forgiveness comes in different forms and degrees and when a couple decides to rekindle through forgiveness it can mean different things to the wife than it does to the husband. The wife usually needs to forgive the husband for taking her for granted, for making her feel like he was simply along for the ride and for not contributing to the function of the family. The husband usually forgives his wife for the hurtful words that she has said and for having a nagging and negative nature. *In the art of forgiveness it is usually harder to forgive words than actions.*

People are much more merciful to forgive the physical wrongs that another person does. This is not uncommon because society assumes that people are going to make mistakes through their life journeys. But there is a common belief that what a person says verbally is usually what that person actually means; *that a person would have not said it if that person did not really mean it on some level.* We have the tendency to never forget the hurtful words that others say, *but it is fairly easier for a person to erase the memory of what he or she has not done in the past by doing what he or she needs to do.* Within time the focus and the memory of the person will be on the new person he or she has become, not the old one.

Stages of Outgrowth

There are four stages that relationships go through during times of transition and outgrowth. Although the length of time and the phases can vary depending on the circumstances and personality types of the married couple, most relationships never completely avoid all four of these stages.[1]

♦ **The Blahs:** This is the stage when you recognize that there is a problem. You start realizing that something is wrong in your relationship and you begin having periods of sadness and confusion or feelings of being hurt. It is not uncommon for a woman to compare her relationship to her friends' and other people's relationships, so it also becomes a time of assessment and evaluation. It is a time of emptiness and relationship discovery.

During this phase there is usually no movement up or down. The problem has already been established in the relationship so things are not usually getting worse but just staying the same. However, it is clear at this point that something is wrong.

It is also common for there to be confusion, because although a woman knows that there is something wrong and that she feels overwhelmed, she also knows that there are some good and valuable qualities in her husband. She is usually torn between what he has become versus the very things that attracted her in the first place.

It is not wise to make any decision about the relationship at this phase. This is the stage of realizing that there is a serious problem. It is too early to decide that the relationship is hopeless and it is too early to believe that deeper and more profound issues will not arise.

♦ **The Break:** This phase involves a period of relationship disgust and confusion. It is the most verbal time for the woman as this is the time when she expresses her unhappiness and is quick to give her opinion. Idle threats and a lack of intimacy are usually the result of this phase. Deep down the wife hopes that her honesty about the imbalance will fix the problem. During this phase her husband is usually shocked by her anger and frustration. He really does not understand completely what she is talking about and why there is such a sudden change in her reaction to him. He feels that he really has not changed much and is essentially the same person but now his wife wants him to become a person he never was in the first place.

This phase will establish how much hurt and how much healing will be needed in the relationship. It is likely that resentment, isolation and hurtful words will be the largest part of this phase. During the time of forgiveness this will be the area that the mercy and forgiveness will play the largest part because this is where most of the hurt takes place.

It is vital that the decision to either rekindle or release the relationship is not made in this phase either. Again, it is still too early to make such an important and final decision. But the most important reason to refrain from decision making in this area is because in this stage the decisions made are solely based on emotion and how the partners are feeling at the time. Caught up in bad feelings and outrage, a woman could completely discount the good things about the husband, the part of the relationship that is worth saving and the consequences of the final decision to leave.

♦ **The Blues:** Many times when partners think that imbalance is their only problem they can often feel that this phase only exists because of the outgrowth. But in reality, regardless of how strong a relationship is it will go through "the blues" at some time. Every day will not be exciting and full of bliss.

In this stage the wife is usually not as verbal about her dissatisfaction, because she has noticed that her criticisms and nagging have not helped earlier. She starts isolating and separating herself from her husband and now sees herself as the one who will have to carry the load. This can be a very dangerous time because this is the stage when a husband can lose the emotional commitment of his wife forever.

The husband, on the other hand, will often be confused during this stage. He feels that at least when his wife was yelling at him he knew where she stood. *At least with angry exchanges he knew that she still cared.* Her new attitude of distance and quietness will either cause him to worry that he has lost her or convince him to do better.

Again, major decisions about the relationship should not be made in this phase, because it too is a time of emotional upheaval. It is important to realize that although the woman tends to be quieter and more isolated, her emotions are governing her personality during this time. It would be easy for her to throw away a salvageable relationship because of her feelings of the blues.

♦ **The Blessings:** What I like to refer to as the freedom. When and how a person gets to this stage is dependent on her or his resentment and how tired she or he is of dealing with the situation. But all relationships that endure outgrowth get to a place of freedom. The depth of this freedom express itself differently with different people. *It is only when you have reached a sense of freedom that is it safe to make a final decision about your relationship.*

If you make the decision to stay, you have now reached the freedom of realizing that you gain more than what you lose when you stay in your relationship. This is the reason why most people decide to rekindle. *Although the redefinition of your "Prince Charming" brings on a whole new meaning, life is better with him than without him.* You understand that although you may have periods of frustration and anger, you can forgive him. Just knowing that what you have is really "not that bad" is a sense of freedom. His making you feel attractive and the fact that he remains loyal and dedicated to the family confirms the need to rekindle and refresh.

If you decide to go you embrace the other part of freedom realizing that you would prefer to be alone than to be with someone who can't contribute to the relationship what you need from him. In this period you recognize that deep-seated anger and resentment are not healthy for you and not fair to him if he is doing the best that he truly knows how to do. The most loving thing in this instance is to "release" the relationship and let it go. *When you realize that his remarrying someone else does not bother you, upset you or concern you but that your lack of concern simply means that you have successfully let go of the emotional part of your relationship, that should be all the confirmation you need to walk away knowing that you have made the best decision for you and for him.*

When it comes to deciding if you are going to release or rekindle it is best to base your decision on your level of peace and allow your peace to define for you the direction in which your freedom lies.

Acknowledgments

I hope that the words in this book have provided insight and that they will ignite your relationships so that they are deeply rooted in friendship and intimacy. In your journey onward my wish for you is that the intensity of the love in your relationships will be more than you have ever expected or experienced.

I want to give special thanks to my husband, Derrick, who has been my biggest fan and friend for twenty-four years of marriage. Thank you for believing in me and taking such special care of me every day. I will be forever grateful for how strongly you believe in my ability to make a difference in the world.

Christian, my son, who is an inspiring writer himself; I could not have asked for a more special, mature and sensitive son. I am proud of the relationship we have developed together. I love you.

My parents, Mr. and Mrs. Joseph Ventus, our relationship has seen both the good and the bad. Thank you for loving me despite myself and I will continue to work hard at making what we have together even more special.

For all of my clients and special friends who believe and follow my work, I thank you for the support and constant love that you have given to me as a speaker and, most importantly, as a person.

Without a doubt, it has been my relationship with God that has given me the confidence, strength and wisdom to accomplish all that I continue to do; for this I will be continually grateful and humbled.

Notes

Chapter 1: Is Your Forty-Two-Year-Old Husband Still Watching Cartoons?

1. Aidan Maconacy, "Superwoman Syndrome: When Best Isn't Good Enough," Ezine Articles, September 2007, http://ezinearticles.com/?Superwoman-Syndrome—-When-Best-Isnt-Good-Enough&id=743091.
2. U.S. Bureau of Labor Statistics, "Wives who earn more than their husbands, 1987-2007," Women in the Labor Force: A Databook Table 25, 2009, http://www.bls.gov/cps/wlftable25.htm.
3. Ygoy.com, "Top Ten Reasons for Divorce," http://women.ygoy.com/top-ten-reasons-for-divorce.
4. Wikipedia, "Platonic love," http://en.wikipedia.org/wiki/Platonic_love.
5. Wikipedia, "Eroticism," http://en.wikipedia.org/wiki/Eroticism.
6. Enotes.com, "Platonic love," http://www.enotes.com/topic/Platonic_love.
7. Wikipedia, "Storge," http://en.wikipedia.org/wiki/Storge.

Chapter 2: Is it the Mother's Fault?

1. U.S. Census Bureau, "Census Bureau Reports Families With Children Increasingly Face Unemployment," January 15, 2010, http://www.census.gov/Press-Release/www/releases/archives/families_households/014540.html.
2. Wikipedia, "Nice guy," http://en.wikipedia.org/wiki/Nice_guy.

Chapter 3: Financial and Infidelity Stressors

1. Bureau of Labor Statistics, "Wives earning more than their husbands, 1987-2006," TED: The Editor's Desk, January 9, 2009, http://www.bls.gov/opub/ted/2009/jan/wk1/art05.htm.

Chapter 4: Deception

[1] Abdul Kargbo, "Who says women mature faster than men?" T'ings 'n Times Blog, May 16, 2007, http://mightyminnow.wordpress.com/2007/05/16/who-says-women-mature-faster-than-men.

[2] "Race and Gender May Play a Role in Survival for the Smallest and youngest Premature Babies," March of Dimes, January 25, 3006, http://www.marchofdimes.com/aboutus/49267_18614.asp.

[3] Henry Campbell Black, "fraud," *Black's Law Dictionary* 6th ed. (St. Paul, MN: West Group, 1999).

[4] Sheri Stritof and Bob Stritof, "How To Tell if Your Spouse is Lying," About.com, http://marriage.about.com/cs/trustissues/a/spotaliar.htm.

Chapter 6: The Secret Rewards of Outgrowing Him

[1] *The Break-Up*, DVD, directed by Peyton Reed (2006; Universal City, CA: Universal Studios).

Chapter 13: Self Reflections

[1] David Popenoe, "Debunking Divorce Myths," Discovery Health, 2002, http://health.discovery.com/centers/loverelationships/articles/divorce.html.

Chapter 17: Looking for a New Mate

[1] Sandra Brown, *How to Spot a Dangerous Man Before You Get Involved* (Alameda, CA: Hunter House, 2005), 214-217.

[2] Ibid., 14-16.

[3] Patricia S. Kuhlman and Gregory A. Kuhlman, "What are the most important factors in marriage success?", Marriage Success Training, 2003, www.statyhitched.com/factors.htm.

[4] F. John Reh, "Pareto's Principle: The 80-20 Rule," About.com, 2010, http://management.about.com/cs/generalmanagement/a/Pareto08 1202.htm.

Chapter 18: Release or Rekindle?

[1] Brian Tome, "Blahs, Break, Blues, and Blessings," in *Free Book* (Nashville, TN: Thomas Nelson Inc, 2010), 125-142.